Mediated Misogynoir

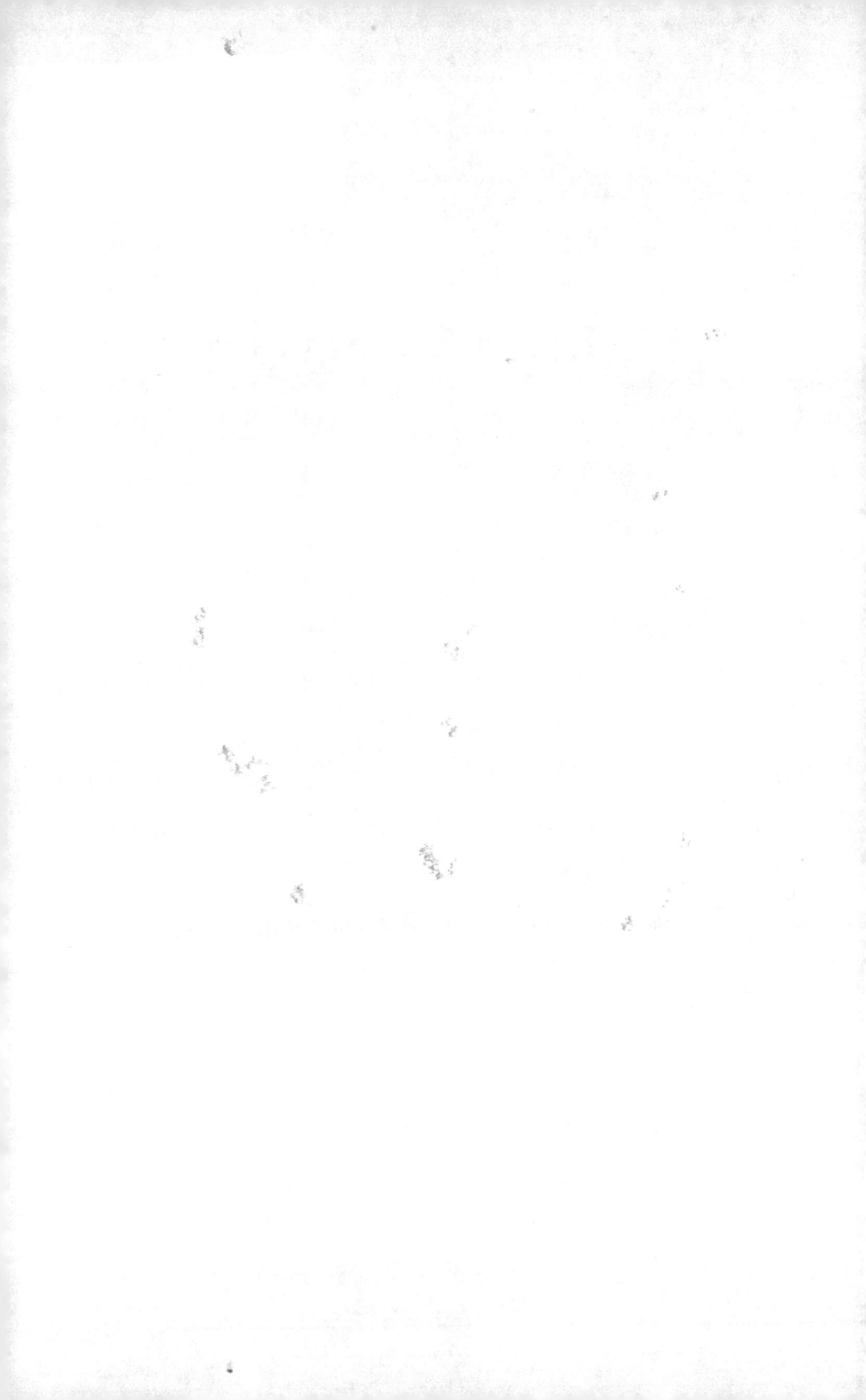

Mediated Misogynoir

Erasing Black Women's and Girls' Innocence in the Public Imagination

Kalima Young

LEXINGTON BOOKS
Lanham • Boulder • New York • London

Published by Lexington Books
An imprint of The Rowman & Littlefield Publishing Group, Inc.
4501 Forbes Boulevard, Suite 200, Lanham, Maryland 20706
www.rowman.com

86-90 Paul Street, London EC2A 4NE

British Library Cataloguing in Publication Information Available

Library of Congress Cataloging-in-Publication Data

Names: Young, Kalima, 1975- author.
  Title: Mediated misogynoir : erasing Black women's and girls' innocence in
    the public imagination / Kalima Young.
  Description: Lanham : Lexington Books, [2022] | Includes bibliographical
    references and index. | Summary: "Mediated Misogynoir: Erasing Black
    Women's and Girls' Innocence in the Public Imagination interrogates
    contemporary media culture to illuminate the ways the intersections of
    anti-blackness and misogyny, i.e., misogynoir, converge to obscure
    public perception of Black women and girls as people with any claim to
    innocence"-- Provided by publisher.
  Identifiers: LCCN 2022015367 (print) | LCCN 2022015368 (ebook) | ISBN
    9781793606631 (cloth) | ISBN 9781793606655 (paperback) | ISBN
  9781793606648 (ebook)
  Subjects: LCSH: African American women in social media. | Social
    media--United States. | African American women in popular
    culture--United States. | Misogynoir--United States. | African American
    women--Social conditions.
  Classification: LCC PN4565.A47 Y68 2022 (print) | LCC PN4565.A47 (ebook)
    | DDC 302.23089/96073--dc23
  LC record available at https://lccn.loc.gov/2022015367
  LC ebook record available at https://lccn.loc.gov/2022015368

Dedication
To my mom, Thomasina, whose answer to my endless
questions as a child was, "Look it up!"

Contents

Acknowledgments

It takes a village to complete any piece of intellectual or creative labor. Thank you to the American Studies doctoral program at the University of Maryland, College Park for guiding me in conducting interdisciplinary scholarship. To the staff, volunteers, and my residency mates at the Blue Mountain Center for providing the beautiful space, time and fellowship needed to bring my first draft to fruition. To Antonia Randolph for inviting me to serve on a panel at the National Women's Studies Association conference where I first articulated the concept of mediated misogynoir. Thanks to the beautiful and fierce circle of feminist and womanist scholars I have had the pleasure to learn from and be inspired by over the years. Thank you to the Electronic Media and Film Department at Towson University for equally supporting my media studies scholarship and creative work. I am incredibly grateful to my friends and creative partners who have generously listened, supported, and cheered me on over the years. Thanks to my siblings Josie, Jimmy, and Trish for being my oldest and most grounding allies. A loving thank-you to my ancestors who have ascended but keep my back straight and my steps firm.

Finally, thank you to my brilliant wife and forever editor, Francine Housier, whose intelligence, encouragement, and unwavering commitment to doing what is right in the world inspires me to try my best every single day.

Introduction

Innocence is often thought of as a state of simplicity and purity. To be considered innocent is to be viewed as vulnerable to harm and worthy of protection from harm. An innocent person's pain is recognized, acknowledged, and addressed. The notion of the innocent child has been hotly contested by religious and philosophical thought-makers for centuries. Are children pure or inherently evil? Are they empty vessels to be filled with lessons that usher them into a world of productive citizenship? Are they bastions of impulse and ego that need a firm, morally righteous hand to steer them straight? At its core, childhood is not an organic process, it is a construction shaped by social forces (James, Jenks, and Prout, 2014, 33). Society decides when a child is a child and when a child is an adult, and much of that decision hinges on the child's perceived innocence. The social forces that create the concept of Black female childhood and the perception of innocence are complicated by embedded racism and sexism.

As a young girl coming of age in West Baltimore, I wrestled with what I now understand is the concept of knowing. Growing up in an impoverished community with three siblings, under the hand of a fiercely intelligent but depressed single mother, I knew a lot. I knew what streets I should not walk down. I knew whose parents worked during the day and whose parents received assistance from the government. I knew all the words to "Paul Revere" from the Beastie Boys' *License to Ill*, as well as all the dance moves in Michael Jackson's *Thriller* video. Every Halloween, our elementary school held a costume parade where the children wore their costumes to school. My family was very poor, and my siblings and I knew not to ask my mother for money to buy something as frivolous as a Halloween costume. That Halloween, my older sister and I decided to dress up like the prostitutes we had seen on television shows like *Starsky and Hutch* and other city-based crime shows. Our fashion designs were also influenced by our favorite band, The Mary Jane Girls. I viewed these TV characters and entertainers as powerful, independent women who said exactly what was on their minds. I wore a blue miniskirt, fishnet fingerless "gloves" made from pantyhose donated by my mother, and my hair was pulled into an updo. In the line for the parade, when we were tasked with announcing our identities, I earnestly told my teacher that I was a hooker. What I read from her expression was a combination of pity, judgment, and consternation. My sister and I were told to step out of the parade line and change clothes. I remember looking back at my teachers as we walked away, seeing their shared glances of disgust and suspicion. We had crossed the line. In their eyes, we were no longer innocent.

Mediated Misogynoir: Erasing Black Women's and Girls' Innocence in the Public Imagination interrogates contemporary media culture to illuminate the ways the intersections of anti-blackness and misogyny, i.e., misogynoir, converge to obscure public perceptions of Black women and girls as people with any claim to innocence. A unique form of hatred, Moya Bailey created the phrase "misogynoir" in 2008 and began using the term online to explain her fatigue with misogyny in hip-hop (Cooper, Morris, Boylorn 2017, 317). While misogyny is generally understood as a hatred of women, *misogynoir* refers to the confluence of racism and sexism Black women and girls experience culturally, socially, and institutionally. For example, in "Misogynoir in Medical Media: On Caster Semenya and R. Kelly," Bailey explores the real-life impact of misogynoir by explaining how the biomedical knowledge produced by physicians constructs certain bodies as normal and others as pathological (2016). Recent revelations about the life-threatening birthing experience of Serena Williams (2018) not only illustrate the consequences of medical misogynoir on Black women's health, but also the ways misogynoir travels across class. Bailey says, "for me, naming misogynoir was about noting both a historical anti-Black misogyny and a problematic intra-racial gender dynamic that had wider implications in popular culture. Misogynoir can come from Black men, white men and women, and even other Black women" (2018). Misogynoir is a useful framework for analyzing the ways white women and Black men use sexism and racism to harm Black women. In 2012, Trudy aka @thetrudz began using the term to describe the impact of misogynoir on her personal life on her blog, *Gradient Lair*. She wanted to show how:

> misogynoir impacts Black women's lives in interpersonal, social, and institutional ways. Although the term is new, the experiences and the histories of Black women are not, and it became important to me to bridge this truth through discussing misogynoir and its impact on things such as street harassment, domestic violence, labor, media/pop culture, State violence, and more. It also became important to me to connect how misogynoir in interpersonal relationships is impacted by misogynoir in mainstream media, which impacts misogynoir and State violence. Making these connections between relationships, entertainment,

and institutional violence helped me not only understand my own experiences but how Black women in particular experience inequalities and abuse. (2018)

As a scholar of Black trauma and media, I liken misogynoir to a needle that is pressed against an acupuncture point—the sites of trauma that are frequently felt by Black women and girls but are often indescribable due to the overlapping threads of oppression we experience. According to Bailey and Trudy, misogynoir has gained its usage within a densely populated online digital environment (2018), which makes it a vitally important tool to discuss the erasure of Black women's and girls' innocence in the public imagination, where media spectacle and surveillance influence our everyday lives.

Information that comes to us through television, movies, photography, music, radio, broadcast, and the internet are mediated texts. Mediated texts shape the way we see the world. Circulating images of Black American pain, wounding, and death through media has been integral in the ongoing fight for civil rights and social justice. For example, on September 15, 1955, *Jet*, a national Black magazine, printed the image of Emmitt Till's battered, disfigured corpse on its cover. This now-iconic image sparked outrage and disgust among Black Americans across the country. Mamie Till Mobley, Emmitt Till's mother, gave *Jet* permission to print the image of her murdered son. This image and its usage reflected the signature civil rights tactic of the Southern Christian Leadership Conference, which was to use Southern atrocity with graphic images of black physical suffering and disseminating those images through multiple media outlets (Torres 2003). Images such as Emmitt Till's corpse are visual testimony of Black pain, wounding, and death. Black pain, wounding, and death imagery has also been used for racial control and subjugation via nineteenth- and twentieth-century lynching photography, and this same type of imagery has also been catalyzed for Black liberation purposes, as in the case of the photos and film of Black citizens in Birmingham, Alabama, being attacked by police dogs and sprayed with high-pressure fire hoses. These images helped spur anti-segregation and voting rights activism in the mid-twentieth century Black American civil rights movement. In the 1980s television, Black pain, wounding, and death imagery proliferated in news reports about criminality in Black communities and through reality television shows such as *Cops*. In 1991, video footage of Rodney King's beating at the hands of Los Angeles police was quickly broadcast via television news reports. With the advent of the Internet, video interviews of traumatized Black Americans have been manipulated into auto-tuned jingles, exemplified by Antoine Dodson's outraged testimony of his 2010 home invasion.

Contemporary videos capturing U.S. police officers killing Black Americans have forced many to acknowledge the disproportionate numbers of Black Americans who are targeted by state violence. These videos have spurred civil rights protests in cities across the nation, including Ferguson, Missouri, and Baltimore, Maryland, and have galvanized online social movements such as the Movement for Black Lives. Yet, when pained images of Black female, queer or disabled bodies appear on our televisions, laptops, and cellular phones, the sociopolitical responses are different and telling, not only in their lack of urgency but also in their limited ability to be read with an intersectional analysis.

OPERATIONALIZING MEDIATED MISOGYNOIR

On January 26, 2020, the world was rocked by the news that retired NBA player Kobe Bryant and his daughter Gianna were among nine people killed when a helicopter crashed into a hillside in Calabasas, California. The passengers were on their way to the Mamba Sports Academy in Thousand Oaks for a basketball game where Gianna was expected to play, and Bryant was expected to coach. Their deaths prompted a familiar cycle of cultural memory-making and collective Black mourning. For Black and Native populations, American ideals of freedom, individualism, democracy, and collective citizenship run counter to the historical reality of America as a country formed by the systematic denial of freedom, uneven citizenship status and selective exclusion from democratic ideals. As a result, historical trauma theorists believe Black and Native Americans suffer from states of historical unresolved grief and disenfranchised grief. Black cultural memory-making and mourning practices are shaped in response to this ongoing grieving process. Public death is so common that Black communities have, "worked this experience into the culture's iconography and included it as an aspect of black cultural sensibility" (Holloway 2002, 3). Black mourning is a collective experience, expressed through community rituals and memorializing narratives. In this spectacular age of relentless media convergence and surveillance, Black collective mourning occurs through shares and retweets, in private and public conversations, in the creation of memorial T-shirts and ephemera and through hyper-local memorials that range from renaming public spaces to retiring an athlete's jersey. This collective Black mourning process is further complicated when the dead are upheld as examples of racial progress and racial greatness.

For many, Kobe Bryant was a larger-than-life icon in the field of professional basketball. For some Black men in particular, Bryant was a cultural hero. He leapt from high school to professional basketball to win five championships with the Lakers, snag two Olympic gold medals and win an Academy Award by transforming a poem to announce his retirement into an animated short film (*Dear Basketball*) that he wrote and narrated. Bryant is an example of what Nicole Fleetwood deems a racial icon. A racial icon is, "both a venerated and denigrated figure [who] function[s] as a visual embodiment of American history and as proof of the supremacy of American democracy" (2015, 8). At various points in his career, Bryant was someone to abhor and to worship. He represented the possibility of transcending both Black economic oppression and the threat of the carceral system. Bryant was charged with felony sexual assault in 2003 stemming from an incident at a Colorado hotel in which Bryant was accused of raping a 19-year-old woman who worked at the property as a front-desk clerk. Prosecutors eventually dropped the case when the woman told them she was unwilling to testify. Bryant later issued an apology, saying he understood that the woman, unlike himself, did not view their encounter as consensual. A lawsuit the woman brought against Bryant was later settled out of court. That Bryant was able to build such a vibrant career after this assault case was no mean feat.

Common stereotypical descriptors ascribed to Black men in film, television, music videos and news outlets include oversexed, violent, comedic, athletic, imprisoned, sexual brutes, magically wise and bestial. Reinforced by media spectacle, these stereotypes create a box that limits the range in which Black men can express their sexual experiences. Bolstered by the historical inability for Black people to define and own their sexuality, these perceptions force Black men to act out in ways that seem to support the stereotype of hyper aggressive sexuality. This is evidenced in the content of R&B and Hip-Hop songs that focus on Black male heterosexual domination. Anthropologist Helan Page (1997) examines Black male media imagery and notes that mass media:

> encourages the viewing public to believe that only a few exceptionally embrace-able African American men are capable of succeeding, while the rest should be contained (literally and figuratively) because they are innately incapable and tend to fail even when offered a chance. (3)

To Page, Black male "embraceabilty and unembracebility" in mainstream media is especially powerful when our attention is drawn to the "unsavory aspects of [Black men's] private or public behavior" (5). Kobe Bryant's very public sexual assault case exemplifies this embraceability politic. For many, Bryant was able to transcend the state of unembracebility that came with the sexual assault case. One of the key elements in reforming Bryant's embraceability was his relationship with his wife, Vanessa, whom he married immediately following the dismissal of the assault charge. Over the years his embraceability was further solidified when the media highlighted the unwavering support he showed to his daughter Gianna, a budding professional basketball player in her own right.

As a racial icon, Kobe Bryant's tragic and sudden death ensured there would be a cycle of public grieving and memorialization meant to solidify the meaning of his life and legacy in the public imagination. Two days after his death, Sports Center anchor Ellen Duncan tearfully relayed an interaction she had with Bryant in which he talked about his intense love and support for his daughters, referring to himself as a "girl dad." Following this emotional retelling, the hashtag #GirlDad began trending on social media. Black men began posting pictures of themselves with their daughters, highlighting their intense love for Black girls and their pride at rearing them. It was an emotional viral display of support for Black girls and a celebration of Black male parenting, both extremely rare in an environment that positions Black girls as troublesome and Black fathers as absent. However, as a public figure and racial icon, Kobe Bryant's unembraceable moments are a matter of public record. It was only a matter of time before a journalist would attempt to weave them into the memorialization and legacy creation that was forming. Through this attempt, a case study in mediated misogynoir became available.

CBS journalist, Gayle King interviewed Lisa Leslie, a former WNBA player and longtime friend of Kobe Bryant. King's interview with Leslie was a full overview of the impact of Kobe Bryant on the sports industry and an intimate look at his relationships with friends and family. When King asked Leslie if she thought the 2003 rape allegations against Bryant complicated the NBA legend's legacy, the following exchange took place:

King: It's been said that his legacy is complicated because of a sexual assault charge, which was dismissed in 2003, 2004. Is it complicated for you as a woman, as a WNBA player?

Leslie: It's not complicated for me at all. Even if there's a few times that we've been at a club at the same time, Kobe's not the kind of guy—never been, like, you know, 'Lis, go get that girl, or tell her or send her this.' I have other NBA friends that are like that. Kobe was never like that. I just never, have ever seen him being the kind of person that would do something to violate a woman or be aggressive in that way. That's just not the person that I know.

King: But Lisa, you wouldn't see it, though. As his friend, you wouldn't see it.

Leslie: And that's possible. I just don't believe that. And I'm not saying things didn't happen. I just don't believe that things did happen with force.

King: Is it even a fair question to talk about it considering he's no longer with us and that it was resolved? Or is it really part of his history?

Leslie: I think that the media should be more respectful at this time. It's like if you had questions about it, you had many years to ask him that. I don't think it's something that we should keep hanging over his legacy. I mean, it went to trial.

King: Yeah, well, the case was dismissed because the victim in the case refused to testify. So, it was dismissed.

Leslie: And I think that that's how we should leave it. (CBS 2020)

CBS used this snippet online to promote the full interview to viewers. As a result, celebrities and fans began to weigh in on the significance of the assault case on Bryant's "legacy" and on the appropriateness of bringing it into conversation so soon after his death. Many took issue with both. Respected rapper, Snoop Dogg (Calvin Broadeus Jr.) took to Instagram to say,

> Gayle King, you're out of pocket for that shit. Way out of pocket. What do you gain from that? We expect more from you, Gayle. Don't you hang out with Oprah [Winfrey]? Why are you all attacking us? We're your people. You ain't come at Harvey Weinstein asking those dumb ass questions . . . I'm sick of y'all. I want to call you one, is it okay if I call her one? Funky doghead bitch. How dare you try and tarnish my homeboy's reputation, punk motherfucker. Respect the family and back off bitch before we come get you. (Newsweek 2020)

Other high profile Black male celebrities were quick to co-sign the rapper's response. NBA player LeBron James, a close friend of Bryant tweeted, "Protect @LisaLeslie at all costs! You're a real Superhero!! Sorry you had to go through that s*%#!!! We are our own worst enemies! #Mamba4Life." Fellow rapper, 50cent tweeted, "I apologize for his language in advance, to people who get distracted by words and miss the point. @SnoopDogg expressing how he feels about Gale & Orpah funky Dog Face LOL #starzgettheapp #abcforlife #lecheminduroi #bransoncognac" (Newsweek 2020). In response to the backlash, Gayle King took to Instagram to explain her position, saying,

> I know that if I had only seen the clip that you saw, I'd be extremely angry with me too. I am mortified, I am embarrassed, and I am very angry . . . Unbeknownst to me, my network put up a clip from a very wide-ranging interview, totally taken out of context, and when you see it that way, it's very jarring. I was advised to say nothing but felt that wasn't 'good enough. (Newsweek 2020)

Throughout this process of back-and-forth volleys, people took to social media and blogs to weigh-in, either supporting Gayle King with hashtags followed by the hashtag #StandwithGale. After a week of discourse over social media, the blogosphere, and news outlets, Snoop Dogg issued a full apology to Gayle King, stating:

> I publicly tore you down by coming at you in a derogatory manner based off emotions of me being angry at questions that you asked . . . . I should have

handled it way different than that . . . I was raised way better than that, so I would like to apologize to you publicly for the language that I used and calling you out of your name and just being disrespectful. I didn't mean for it to be like that. I was just expressing myself for a friend that wasn't here to defend himself. I apologize. (NYT 2020)

This entire scenario, from Gayle King's interview to the final apology from Snoop Dogg, illuminates "mediated misogynoir." Mediated misogynoir considers the role of media and spectacle in enabling the racism and sexism Black women and girls experience. For a situation to exemplify mediated misogynoir, there must exist 1) a broad circulation of the text (viral video, clip, film, television, blog post, etc.) in a mediated environment; 2) a discourse that calls to question Black women and girls' full citizenship and complex personhood and 3) an overreliance on media as the vehicle by which people measure Black racial progress and garner racial justice.

CIRCULATION OF THE TEXT

In a mediated environment, the words and deeds of Black women and girls are rapidly circulated through online platforms (Twitter, Facebook, Instagram, blogs, and podcasts) as well as traditional media outlets (news, print, television, radio, movies). The hyper-circulation of Black female thought often leads to online discourses that flatten, obscure, and dismiss Black women's valid critiques of the world. At times, this hyper-circulation results in an excess of cyberaggression. Cyberaggression "allows bystanders to interact with direct conversations [online], and [participate in] broad negative behaviors, such as racism and misogyny" (Francisco and Felmlee 2019, 5). The cyberaggression of Snoop Dogg and his supporters was meant to uphold specific social norms and hierarchies. The United States is structured by a White supremacist, capitalist, patriarchy (hooks 1997, 6) that places White men at the top of the social hierarchy. This worldview manifests in U.S. domestic and international policies, as well as in the media the U.S. creates and distributes. In Black communities, this heteropatriarchal standpoint is often preserved by placing the needs of Black men at the forefront of Black social justice movements and using Black male success, such as the presidential election of Barak Obama in 2008, as a barometer to gauge Black racial progress.

COMPLEX PERSONHOOD

Cyberaggression is often a response to Black female critiques of Black male words and actions. Calling Gayle King a "funky dog-head bitch" is undeniably misogynistic but what is more telling is the rapper's laments, "we expect more from you," and "Why are you all attacking us? We're your people." This sentiment is also apparent in LeBron James's, "we are our own worst enemies." Collective identity is the perception of a shared status or relation (Owens 2003). In their moments of bombastic volley, Snoop Dogg and LeBron call on a collective "we" mean Black people, specifically Black men, as an aggrieved population. Snoop Dogg takes it upon himself to assume other Black people do not want to engage in the question of Kobe Bryant's legacy and his sexual assault charge. His laments make assumptions about both Gayle King's racial loyalty and the concerns of Black people. By pitting Gayle King against a collective we, Snoop and his supporters deny her any evidence of complex personhood. Avery Gordon (1997) defines complex personhood as a "rich contradictory subjectivity" (4); one that factors into the stories we tell about ourselves and the actualities of our lived experiences. Complex personhood ascribes individuals a sense of a collective "we" while also acknowledging how individual, contradictory, and subjective our experiences are, even within the "we." As she poses, "complex personhood means that the stories people tell about themselves, about their troubles, about their social worlds, and about their society's problems are entangled and weave between what is immediately available as a story and what their imaginations are reaching toward" (6). By implying Gayle King is betraying the race i.e., Black men, King becomes a bad actor in whatever imagined story the rapper is reaching for as he mourns his hero, Kobe Bryant. Snoop Dogg is not the only one denying a Black woman complex personhood in this story. It would be remiss not to mention LeBron James' assertion that WNBA player, Lisa Leslie must be protected from Gayle King and her racial betrayal. With his, "@"Protect @LisaLeslie at all costs! You're a real Superhero!!" James literally assumes Lisa Leslie was being attacked and that her honor needed to be defended. This completely contradicts the tone of the exchange between King and Leslie, in which both women respectfully hold their own.

Additionally, Snoop et al., places a burden of responsibility on Gayle King as a journalist. Black reporters played a crucial role before and during the height of the civil rights movement. They risked their lives and acted as a go-between for the Black community and the White mainstream media (Gilliam 2018). The long tradition of Black journalist as the spokespersons for Black communities within mainstream media also places an undo restriction on Black reporters' ability to critique Black communities. As Soraya

Nadia McDonald says, "If you're a black woman journalist writing about black men, it's not unusual to be accused of some sort of racial betrayal," (Daily News 2020). This is a common tactic in the U.S. where the responsibility of "racial uplift often falls disproportionally on Black women" (Morris, Kahlor, 2018, 573). One need only look at the 1960's War on Poverty doctrine to recognize how Black women are regularly held responsible for Black poverty, failures in public education, health disparities, and Black incarceration rates (Collins, 2005). With the responsibility of racial uplift on their shoulders, Black women have fought hard to navigate what Melissa Harris-Perry calls a sexual dissemblance. In the early twentieth century, dissemblance was borne out of a politics of respectability whereby Black women's "ability to work on behalf of black communities and to demand fair, just treatment from the state rested on their sterling moral character" (Harris-Perry 2011,15). This has effectively meant that Black female sexual politics must always balance the fight against perceptions of Black hypersexuality and the very complex, often messy reality of Black women's sexual lives. Contemporarily, this sexual dissemblance often makes it difficult for Black women to navigate "public moments of intra-racial sexual anxiety" (16) such as Kobe Bryant's sexual assault charge. It is often better to remain quiet about Black sexuality or err on the side of minimizing the sexual harms visited upon Black women, especially when those harms occur at the hands of Black men. By publicly speculating about Kobe Bryant's moment of unembracebility, Gayle King was effectively eschewing her assumed duty as a Black woman to "unconditionally support and defend Black men" (Morris, Kahlor 2018, 573); making her journalistic inquiry an actual "attack" on Black people; specifically, men. By asking, "why are you all attacking us?" the rapper positions Gayle King amongst two groups that cannot fully be trusted by Black men: Black women who step out of line and a media culture that harms Black men for profit.

MEDIA CULTURE AND RACIAL PROGRESS

Media culture shapes the ways mediated misogynoir appears. Media culture refers to the overall impact and intellectual guidance exerted by mass media on the public. Mass media and the culture that is created to support it helps us fashion our sense of reality. The gatekeepers of mass media exert a powerful influence over every aspect of our lives, from our politics to the way we structure our families. Sociologist Pierre Bourdieu suggests three different types of capital comprise the structure of society. Economic capital simply refers to economic resources, such as cash and property. Social capital refers to the resources and advantages we get from the groups we belong to and the people we know. Cultural capital refers to more symbolic elements that signal our class position, such as our tastes, skills, mannerisms, and credentials (Swartz 1998). To be deemed successful in media culture is to acquire all three types of capital.

In the eyes of Snoop Dogg, Gayle King's behavior is even more egregious because of her proximity to gatekeepers of ever powerful media culture. Gayle King has been in television journalism for over forty years. Through her relationship with Black media mogul, Oprah Winfrey and CBS, Gayle King's words and deeds are hypervisible in a mediated space. CBS's weekday morning shows earn more revenue than its news programming (Koblin 2020) making Gayle King one of the most powerful and influential anchors on the network. After the departure of Charlie Rose and CEO Leslie Moonves from the network due to sexual harassment allegations, CBS rebranded itself with Gayle King as the "de facto face of CBS News" (*Hollywood Reporter* 2019, 52). When King talks to or about Black men, her actions are hypervisible. This is partially due to the praise she received after her 2019 interview with former R & B singer and convicted child sex offender, R. Kelly. During the interview, as the singer became increasingly erratic, and volatile, Gayle King remained calm, inquisitive, and unimpressed. The interview went viral due to its spectacular elements. First, R. Kelly, a figure who had managed to avoid public accountability for his crimes, was disintegrating *on air* due to his own narcissism. Secondly, even though she was simply doing her job as a journalist, Gayle King successfully portrayed the strong Black woman who is unimpressed by male egoism trope, a familiar narrative in our popular imagination. Finally, liveness is the "assertion that television representation has a privileged claim to immediacy and transparency" (Torres 2003, 50). R. Kelly's unpredictability certainly lived up to the burden of liveness, which helped the interview feel both authentic and intimate. The praise Gayle King received about her handling of the interview, as well as the fact that her annual salary doubled following its airing, solidified her as an anchor who is hard-hitting and a ratings giant.

Discussing the hypervisibility of Black women in public discourse, Tamika Carey posits the "racist logic of [Black] surveillance [has] conditioned hostile publics to read outspoken or critical black women as thinking 'too highly' of themselves or moving beyond their designated boundaries" (Carey 2017, 143). Snoop Dogg and his supporters attempted to put Gayle King back in her place at the bottom of the Black social hierarchy by using mediated misogynoir. In this way, mediated misogynoir is a manifestation of a politic of containment (Collins 1998) wherein Black women are controlled, monitored, and scrutinized through mediated texts which act as surveillance tools.

Media representation aids a belief in racial progress that is often out of alignment with the real, lived experiences of Black people. A 2017 study found that, "Americans, on average, systematically overestimate the extent to which society has progressed toward racial economic equality, driven largely by overestimates of current racial equality" (Krause et al., 2017, 10324). Within this paradigm, America's deliberate racial segregation has concrete consequences for Black and white Americans. Segregation ensures that Black Americans experience "heightened exposure to environmental hazards, relegation to under-resourced schools, increased and continued surveillance by law enforcement and eventual death" (Gilliam et al., 2002, 755). Sociologists studying racial proximity contend that, "the persistence of racial segregation means that impersonal influences such as the media are likely to play a significant role in the development of racial attitudes" (Martin et al., 2017). Segregation ensures most interactions non-Black people have with Black Americans occur through mediated representation. Reliance on mediated representations of Black life opens the gateway to contested definitions of Blackness. Blackness is always in constant conversation with itself, defined not just by what Black people see as authentic and familiar but also, "in stark difference against that which it is not" (Madison, DeFrantz, Gonzales 2014, 4). If Blackness is based on representations of Blackness, when "white-identified subjects perform 'black' signifiers—normative or otherwise—the effect is always already entangled in the discourse of otherness" (Johnson 2003, 4).

Access to mass media is often held up as evidence of racial progress. Kobe Bryant, Snoop Dogg, Gayle King, 50cent, LeBron James and Lisa Leslie all owe their success to media culture. Mass media circulates their images, positioning them as celebrities and icons. Lisa Leslie is evidence of gender equality as one of the superstars of the WNBA. Snoop and 50cent are legends in Hip-Hop. Kobe Bryant and LeBron James are superheroes in the NBA. Gayle King is the face of a network. As celebrities and icons, these figures are a part of the system and, as Black Americans, they are apart from the system because it relies on misrepresentation for its success. Critiquing the hegemony of visual culture, Hallas and Guerin suggest "for all our reliance on images, we never quite believe in their revelations. Despite the privilege given to the authority and presence of the image, it was after all, just an image, a picture" (2007, 10). When the authenticity of the visual testimony is discredited, such as the police beating of Rodney King captured on video, the distinction between seeing (the moment of recognition) and reading (the moment of conclusion) comes into consideration. The Rodney King video seemed to capture an undeniable truth of police brutality but was discredited due to several cultural implications for how we read images of Black male bodies in pain. Tackling white paranoia in response to the Rodney King video, Judith Butler establishes a difference between "seeing" and "reading" video evidence. She argues, "when the visual is fully schematized by racism, the 'visual evidence' to which one refers will always and only refute the conclusions based upon it; for it is possible within this racist episteme that no black person can seek recourse to the visible as the sure ground of evidence" (1993, 20). In her estimation, the visual field cannot be neutral to questions of racism and White supremacy. I would also argue, it cannot be neutral to sexism either.

If, as schema theory notes, messages are filtered through understood "truths," differing schemas detract from the "truthfulness" of images circulating in mass media. This contradictory relationship with media culture shapes mediated misogynoir. Access to media culture signals success; yet it is that same access which cause Black women and girls to be misread in mediated spaces. It is this access that allowed Gayle King to be held up as a hero for her interview with R. Kelly, and then declared a race betrayer by questioning Kobe Bryant's legacy. It is that same access that allows Black women's intellect to thrive via social media without having to cite the actual Black women who created the theories. It is in this complicated, contradictory space that mediated misogynoir gains traction.

ERASING BLACK INNOCENCE

A recent report by the Center on Poverty and Equity at Georgetown Law has collected data showing that "adults view Black girls as less innocent and more adult-like than their white peers, especially in the age range of 5–14" (Epstein, Blake, and Gonzales 2019, 1). The report modifies the term "adultification" to refer to "perception of Black girls as more adult, without reference to their individual behaviors" (4). Adultification comes with detrimental consequences for Black girls' health, scholastic achievement, sexuality, and psychological well-being. It also increases Black girls' chances of encountering the carceral system and experiencing gender-based violence. If Black girls are seen as needing less protection, nurturing and support, they are also assumed to know more about adult topics, such as sex. The adultification of Black children can be traced back to Black experiences of colonization and enslavement. Black children experienced the same dehumanizing and demeaning practices as their adult counterparts. In visual culture, icons provide representations of reality. Regardless of age, Black female bodies have always served as "an icon for Black sexuality" (Gilman 1985, 285). One need only look to imagery from the minstrelsy era to glean society's perception of Black children as both disposable and overtly sexual.

Epstein, Blake, and Gonzales surveyed over 325 adults, 74 percent of whom were white females. Their report is a timely and urgent call to action to improve the livelihood of Black girls across multiple public systems. Yet, the teachers who served my sister and me "knowing" looks were all Black women. As a scholar of race and gender-based trauma and Black identity formation, I wonder about the way Black adult men and women "adultify" Black girls. What are the consequences of the adultification of Black girls by those who share their racial identity and history? How is the magic or nimbleness of Black girls complicated by their adultification? Videos of little Black girls illustrating a level of dance technique beyond their years, or perfectly parroting adult Black women go viral regularly, earning the #blackgirlmagic hashtag. There is something awe-inspiring in those moments where little Black girls know their power. Yet, their ability to wield that power often strips them of the protections readily provided to more "innocent" i.e., white, children. How does this adultification hinder and help Black girls survive a heterosexist, white supremacist, and capitalist system?

Black feminist scholars have worked exhaustively to pin down the nature of Black women's and girls' modes of survival. In *Fierce Angels: The Strong Black Woman in American Life and Culture*, Sheri Parks traces the development of the strong Black woman archetype through historical myths to the present. Exploring Black mothers' responses to the violent, public death of their children, Parks suggests Black women show compassionate intelligence, fierce love, persistence, personal resiliency, and nimbleness (2013). The concept of "nimbleness," Black women's constant navigation between gender, race, and caste, speaks to an interior process of negotiation with outside and inner perceptions. In her formidable book of essays *When Chickenheads Come Home to Roost: A Hip-Hop Feminist Breaks It Down*, Joan Morgan writes of being inspired to "to recapture the feminine and discover the fierceness of a black girl's magic" (2017, 6). Hers is a battle cry to reclaim and celebrate the unique power of the Black feminine, a black girl's magic. A true black girl's magic is about the resiliency and hard work of Black women and girls despite the external narratives that diminish or overlook them. Black girl magic comes from other Black women seeing and uplifting the accomplishments of their sistas where the white world and Black male patriarchal world abuses and erases them. In *Sister Citizen: Shame, Stereotypes and Black Women in America,* Melissa Harris-Perry uses the metaphor of the crooked room to describe how Black women constantly seek to balance themselves in a room made crooked by distorted gender and racial expectations. The ability to see the full strength, vulnerability and innocence of Black women and girls is critical to understanding Black women's and girls' ability to live, thrive, and fail in a heterosexist, white supremacist, and capitalist system.

DIGITIZING BLACK WOMEN AND
GIRLS: A BRIEF DISCUSSION

This book explores how the twinning of sexism and racism in our public imagination uses multiple forms of media to strip Black women and girls of any claim of innocence. To digitize Black women and girls is to make their experiences central to our understanding of digital media creation, utilization, and consumption on the Internet. The first chapter, Viral Misogynoir, tackles this concept as it specifically relates to digital media and viral videos. It is difficult to offer a singular historical analysis of the Internet's representation of Black women and girls because the realm of the digital, though a newer medium, operates under the same logics undergirding all other forms of mass media. What can be offered in this brief discussion is an examination of the cultural logics undergirding the digital realm, the fields of scholarship that may provide paths for further investigation, and some approaches for recognizing Black women's and girls' digital resistance. The latter two threads will be picked up again in the concluding chapter, The Urgency of Now.

Much has been written about the myths, stereotypes, and archetypes that have followed Black women and girls through every incarnation of popular media text, from literature, visual art, and advertising to music, film, and television. Overall, mass media has been controlled by White male capitalist hegemonies. This White imaginary is informed by colonial logics—those who have been conquered are Othered. Othering takes the form of erasure and dehumanization physically, and culturally. These tactics work to further justify the conquerors' right to exploit the resources of the conquered. In the United States, colonial logics dovetail with frontier theory—the idea that the United States evolved because of the expansion from east to west. By conquering the indigenous (committing genocide) and taming (exploiting) American lands, a unique American national identity and culture was formed. Within nineteenth- and twentieth- century logics, Black women and girls have come to represent Otherness. This is evident throughout Western art and popular culture (Mafe 2018, 5–6). Popular culture representation of Black women and girls ranges from the exploitation of Saartjie Baartman aka the Hottentot Venus, to old film tropes such as the Mammy and the Tragic Mulatto (Bogle 1973/2016). The Mammy, Matriarch, Jezebel, Sapphire, and Welfare Queen further haunts Black women and girls in media representation (Collins 1990/2000). These controlling images have had direct material and political consequences for Black women and girls globally. Regardless of changing mediums and the increased inclusion of Black male and female creatives at the helms of these mediums—objectification, and exploitation of Black women and girls persists (Goldman, Ford, Vanetta 2014, 8). Exploring the links between the nineteenth- century rise of the printing press and the twenty-first-century digital media convergence, Susan Zeigar notes how the cultural habits of mass media consumption impacts humans affectively, psychologically, and socially (2018, 3). Popular media thrives by tapping into our affective world—our embodied response informed by our schemas and our histories. These schemas and histories are rife with distortions of Black women's and girls' humanity.

DIGITAL COLONIALISM

Digital media are any media that twines technology and content. Networking technology was first developed by an array of scientists and engineers from the 1950s to 1995, starting first with improvements in computing spurred by the Cold War. In the 1980s–1990s, the creation of Domain Name Systems (DNS), Transmission Control Protocols (TCP), Internet Protocols (IP) and email increased the traffic of networked computers across the world. By 1995, the Internet and World Wide Web came to popularity with the launch of Netscape Navigator. This graphical web browser and the technology to send huge amounts of many forms of content across the web opened a digital world that has impacted both media making and media consumption.

Scholars of the Internet often note how pre-millennium discourse about the digital age framed the Internet as an almost utopian place of possibility. It was a new frontier, one leaning heavily toward revolution. The Internet was dubbed a world where cyberpunks and hackers operated alongside businesses large and small, all dedicated to a free flow of information and commerce. Lisa Nakamara points out it "is in this moment that the neoliberal discourse of color blindness would become linked with the Clinton-Gore administration's identification of the Internet as a privileged aspect of the national political economy" (3). The Internet was a lighthouse steering travelers toward post-racial lands. Data would be shared. Communities of like-minded people could carve out a space to connect. Role playing games as well as anonymous chat rooms would allow people to try on a myriad of identities, but this new frontier was also intimately entwined with corporate interests. As digital journalist and Pulitzer Prize winner James Ball reminds us, "systems don't build themselves. The internet and the way it works were all human decisions, made by groups of men—it's almost always men—in small rooms, with their own particular ideologies, motivations and divisions" (2020, 3). This new digital frontier was being born while humanities studies scholars were noting, "the residual traces of centuries of axiomatic European domination inform the general culture, the everyday language, and the media, engendering a fictitious sense of the innate superiority of European-derived cultures and peoples" (Shot and Stam 1994/2000, 1). The digital turn—the Internet, World Wide Web and digital media technologies came to the public while the humanities and cultural studies was explicitly focusing on addressing the flaws of Eurocentrism and as multi-culturalism was emerging in academia. At the same time, Black feminism was articulating the lack of a racialized lens in feminist studies and asserting the concept of intersectionality as an intervention. These academic introspections into colonial logics and intersectionality did not bleed into the rhetoric of the new digital frontier of which the Internet was a key component. New frontiers do not exist, they come into being through the meanings we ascribe to them. Can a space largely created and maintained by White male capitalist hegemony ever become a utopia for Black women and girls? The answer to this question is notoriously hard to trace because there is no field solely dedicated to understanding the role of the Internet on the lives of Black women and girls, though the field of Black digital humanities offers some avenues.

BLACK DIGITAL HUMANITIES

Black digital humanities work with Black studies to recover the humanity of Black people who have been stripped of it through globalized racialization (Gallon 2016, 44). This is done by using digital technology to recover lost histories, literary texts, and cultural artifacts across the diaspora. The digital realm has become a space for creation of liberatory projects like the Million Woman March (Everette 2009), #BlackLivesMatter and "Black" Twitter. Black digital humanities create avenues for scholars to recover, archive and critique diasporic Black liberation movements as they expand and change shape, such as DocNow at the Maryland Institute for Technology in the Humanities. Inspired by the archive of tweets generated during the Ferguson Uprising in 2015, DocNow is creating a cloud-ready, open-source application that will be used for collecting tweets and their associated metadata and Web content for future social media activism (MITH 2021). The rich and expanding work of Black genealogy studies also benefits from the work of Black digital humanities processes. Digital humanities often focus on majority culture's engagements with the digital. Black digital humanities insert Blackness into the field of digital humanities which rarely acknowledges Blackness as human (Gallon 2016, 47). Each of these turns in Black digital humanities opens the door for exploration of Black women and girls in the digital realm. Unfortunately, Black digital humanities as it stands does not have arms wide enough to make the digitization of Black women and girls central to the field. Archiving and digitizing is noble work but how can that work be structurally shifted to liberate Black women and girls whose virtual bodies are made into avatars and memes, while their physical bodies are constantly under attack by state violence and surveillance? Algorithms are sets of rules and codes that tell a computer what to do. In her study of algorithmic oppression, Safiya Nobel reminds us that the Internet is neither benign nor neutral. In her investigation of Google's search engine, she found a simple search for "black girls" resulted in images and advertising that hypersexualized them. Codes are created by humans who bring their own biases and schemas to the work. The physical world is replicated in the digital and if big data corporations such as Google continue practices that oppress women and people of color employees, "it will become increasingly difficult for technology companies to separate their systematic and inequitable employment practices, and the far-right ideological bents of some of their employees, from the products they make for the public" (2018, 2). Digital tools and projects actively contribute to global inequality, from voting interference by foreign actors to social media tools that invite voting interference from within.

CENTERING BLACK WOMEN AND GIRLS IN THE DIGITAL

Centering Black women and girls in explorations of the Internet and digital media opens avenues to recognize the ways Black women and girls resist erasure of their vulnerabilities and demand protection from institutionalized misogynoir. Marginalized voices often use the Internet and digital media for activist purposes. As more BIPOC, women, queer and disabled bodies enter the academy, the shape of digital humanities has expanded. Calls for the "case for attention to race, class, gender, sexuality, ability, nationality, and other categories" are contributing to a shift in the field (Risam 2019, 1). How can the field of digital humanities be further pushed to make Black women and girls central in its exploration of the Internet and digital media?

Perhaps we must rip the digital frontier from its colonial origin story. *In Digital Diaspora: A Race for Cyberspace*, Everette posits that the first virtual communities were created from the hold of the slave ship. She uses the concept of African diasporic consciousness as the first virtual space where "[s]evered from the familiar terrain of their homelands and dispatched to the overcrowded bowels of slave vessels, the abducted Africans forged out of necessity a virtual community of intercultural kinship structures and new languages in which to express them" (2009, 2). It may be helpful to liken the cultural flows Black women and girls have crafted online (feminist blogs, online natural hair care communities, hashtag activist campaigns) to the shared, inherited and exchanged survival strategies spread amongst members of the African diaspora across the Black Atlantic (Gilroy 1993). Instead of seeing the Internet as a new frontier to be explored and conquered, perhaps the virtual world is simply an expansion of African diasporic consciousness transformed by computer technology. Additionally, if we frame diaspora as "a space that is neither created nor maintained by heteronormativity" (Williams 2005,10), we can then trace the virtual realm back to Black feminists and Black queer activists who developed ways to explode binaries and essentialist views of Black identity. Recognizing the role Black women have played in creating the technology of the Internet and digital technology is a key intervention in the digitization of Black women and girls as well. Black female engineers and programmers operate in a field informed by logics that do not recognize their humanity. How has their resistance to oppression informed the way digital technology has shifted over time? The Internet and its digital tools are part and parcel of a surveillance society. Scholars studying Black surveillance also have a role to play in the digitizing of Black women and girls as they note what happens when, "blackness, black human life, and the conditions imposed upon it, enter discussions of surveillance" (Browne 2015, 162).

Scholars who are attempting to reorient the Internet to insert Black female and femme humanity choose a myriad of approaches. Moya Bailey's digital alchemy speaks to "the ways women of color, Black women, and Black nonbinary, agender, and gender-variant folks transform everyday digital media into valuable social justice media that recode the failed scripts that negatively impact their lives" (2021, 24). Bailey goes on to showcase the ways these groups have used digital technology to create their own digitized world rather than force themselves to adapt to a colonial digital frontier. Safiya Nobel's continued call to illuminate algorithmic oppression: the racist and sexist ways big data fail people of color and women, is also a worthy tool for inserting Black womens' and girls' humanity into the story of the Internet. Catherine Steele highlights how Black women have long used blogs and other digital community platforms to create new theory and arguments to further social justice (Steele 2021, 2). Steele has also shown how the world of the digital has created a space to see Black joy as resistance (Steel and Lu 2018, 1). Discussing the ways tech journalists fail to engage Black women's experiences the digital, Sydette Harry notes the variety of ways Black women are engaged in tech. She calls attention to the Chenoa Baker's Digital Collage of Representations: 20 Curatorial Instagram Accounts to Follow as an example of the ways Black women are reimagining the digital archive and capturing the things that are ignored or easily forgotten as ephemera of a moment in time (Harry, Wired 2021). The studies and approaches I have touched upon in this brief discussion are avenues to explore if we are to truly understand the digitization of Black women and girls and the fight against mediated misogynoir.

APPROACH

As an interdisciplinary work, *Mediated Misogynoir: Erasing Black Women and Girls' Innocence in the Public Imagination* borrows from the fields of American studies and media studies, using a combination of textual analysis, discourse analysis, and film theory. It is written using a reflexive voice common to Black feminist discourse. Each chapter is grounded in theory and in the personal. "Viral Misogynoir" analyzes viral video encounters between law enforcement officials and Black American women and girls. Starting with a larger articulation of the convergence of misogynoir, surveillance and spectacle, this chapter considers the way misogynoir contributes to the misreading of gender-based violence in public discourse. "Misogynoir and Media Culture," examines the way media culture allows misogynoir to masquerade as Black Representational Progress by unpacking misogynoir in F. Gary Gray's 2015 biopic, *Straight Outta Compton*. "Monstrous Misogynoir" interrogates performances by Gabourey Sidibe in Lee Daniels' *Empire* and Viola Davis in Shonda Rhimes' *How to Get Away with Murder* to argue that both female actors complicate notions of the "hyper-sexualized other" while supporting Barbara Creed's theory of the universal "monstrous feminine." This examination places misogynoir in conversation with the concept of a decolonized screen to consider a corrective method of reading Black women and girls' sexuality in other fictive media narratives. "Surviving Misogynoir" uses dream hampton's 2019 documentary, *Surviving R. Kelly* as a case study of how misogynoir complicates the discourse in Black communities around justice and gender-based violence. By analyzing rhetoric around Black kinship and incest, misogynoir is illustrated as a key factor in complicating Black community response to intra-racial gender-based violence. The final chapter, "The Urgency of Now" reiterates the vital need for new frameworks to understand Black women and girls in media culture and calls for an expansion of the field of Black feminist media studies. This chapter proposes core tenets and methods to guide Black feminist media scholarship and ends with suggestions for combating mediated misogynoir. Combined, these chapters operationalize mediated misogynoir to re-visibilize Black women's and girls' innocence in our public imagination.

Chapter 1

Viral Misogynoir

SPECTACLE AND SURVEILLANCE

In the United States, mediated misogynoir thrives due to a dangerous mix of spectacle and surveillance. Guy Debord suggests that everything that we consume embodies a mixture of distraction and reinforcement that serves to reproduce the capitalist mode of society and economy. He asserts a society of spectacle arises when 1) social life is replaced by mediated representations of life, and 2) uniform narratives are endlessly repeated. Debord's theory sees image saturation (an excess of visual stimuli) as critical to the creation of a spectacle society. A surveillance society is one in which media consumers engage technology that tracks, records, and monitors their everyday lives (Lyon, 2014). Viral videos emerge out of a combination of both a society spectacle and a surveillance society.

Viral videos are a contemporary example of image saturation. A video is perceived to have gone viral based on the total views of the video and the social media spread of the video after its initial release. These videos spread across media platforms because viewers take it in their own hands and share it with their social networks (Guadagno, et al., 2013). The act of "liking" and "sharing" these viral videos might seem to contradict Debord's conception that image saturation fosters passivity, however, there is a difference between explicit participation (producing social media text and artifacts) and implicit participation (sustaining social media connections). Liking and sharing are both explicit and implicit participation (Villi and Matikainen 2016). Social media participation is motivated by users' desires to stay connected to one another and by media companies' desire to connect to users/consumers for data collection that leads to profit. Liking and sharing content is often more about staying plugged into a conversation than actively shaping and molding that conversation (Hogan 2010) for a particular purpose.

Images of immediate and explosive injury are considered spectacular violence (Nixon 2011). The fact that viral videos of Black pain, wounding, and death are moments of spectacular violence contributes to the way these videos travel across social media. Spectacular violence, compounded with the uniformity of the images, and increased image saturation, fosters passive interactions. Mediated spectacular violence committed against Black people often normalizes the systemic cultural and physical violence Black Americans experience in real life. For example, mass-mediated images of roaming young Black men fueled the persecution of the Exonerated Five (formerly referred to as the Central Park Five) in the 1990s (Bumiller 2008). In this environment of image repetition and continuous self-monitoring, the dissemination of images of Black women and girls' pain and oppression are a part of a larger system of impression management that urges media consumers to immediately respond and have an opinion without engaging a deeper structural and intersectional analysis.

BLACK SURVEILLANCE

In the United States, Blackness was made hypervisible during slavery and post-slavery through the slave ships, ledgers, branding, lantern laws and other means of identification. Under surveillance, Black people's "unruliness" has always been used as a way to "mask the violence of the slave trader by displacing the violence of slavery onto the African" (Brown 2015). Surveillance makes it so that even the most "truthful" accounts of injustice against Black people are repeatedly distorted by histories of racist image reading practices, complicating the reliance on dashboard cameras, police body cameras, and Facebook live feeds to garner justice.

Media consumption, media convergence and an affinity for visual culture contribute to a society of spectacle and surveillance where we 1) make what we see, 2) we believe what we see and, 3) what we document with our cellular phones supports *our* specific reading of injustice. This distinction is important because very rarely are law enforcement officers penalized when their violence against Black men, women, and children are caught on camera. Watching and sharing is not the same as seeing and witnessing. *Seeing* is watching an event unfold. It is a manner of discerning what is occurring visually. When light falls on the eyes, a process occurs which stimulates the visual cortex to detect shapes, colors, and motion. Though a complex ocular process, we see. To see does not automatically mean to comprehend. Comprehension comes through the process of reading. *Reading* is a process of filtering what is being seen through one's schema. Video evidence may show the entirety of an incident, but the interpretation of what is being shown changes depending upon how one reads the bodies on screen. Witnessing is a process of seeing and reading the visual from an intention place of empathy.

In October 2015, a viral video emerged of 15-year-old Dajerria Becton being forcibly restrained by police officer Eric Casebolt in what is described as the 'McKinney, TX pool party incident.' Fox news correspondent Megyn Kelly proclaimed Dajerria Becton "was no saint" (MSNBC 2016). Kelly's statement exemplifies mass media's inability to read Casebolt's assault of Becton as gender-based violence. Noting Becton did not follow the officer's warnings, Kelly continued, "I'm sure he didn't know she was 15 at the time." To place this in a visual context, Dajerria Becton was a Black girl with long brown hair and a thin build. She was wearing a bright orange-and-red two-piece bathing suit. She wore no shoes. She was armed only with her skin, her voice, and her indignation. In contrast, Eric Casebolt, 41 years old, was a heavyset white male police officer clad in a black police uniform. He was armed with a service revolver, a utility belt with handcuffs, and the authority to arrest, restrain and wound those on site. In the cell phone footage, Becton is seen walking away after exchanging words with Casebolt. Within three minutes of their interaction, Casebolt forcibly grabs Becton by her arm and hair, drags her across the grass and throws her to the ground. Becton cries for her mother. Casebolt forces her face into the grass and kneels on her exposed back.

I experienced several emotions while witnessing this video. My first reaction was outrage. Then, despite already knowing the outcome of the situation, I felt abject fear about what could happen next. This feeling was followed by the recognition of how intimately and violently entwined Casebolt and Becton's bodies appeared in the frame. I interpreted this assault as gender-based violence. Gender-based violence (GBV) refers to violence that is directed at an individual based on his or her biological sex, gender identity, or perceived adherence to socially defined norms of masculinity and femininity. It includes physical, sexual, and psychological abuse; threats; coercion; arbitrary deprivation of liberty; and economic deprivation, whether occurring in public or private life (USAID 2016). GBV is often unrecognizable in the lives of Black women and girls. In discussing everyday violence in the lives of Black women, Carolyn M. West suggests Black women's bodies are never regarded as under siege but instead, "accessible and able to be abused without consequences" (1995, 166). The statistics support this assessment.

According to the 2010 National Intimate Partner and Sexual Violence Survey, 43.7 percent of non-Hispanic Black women have experienced rape, physical violence, and/or stalking by an intimate partner in their lifetime. Black women experience more lethal GBV and are often less likely to report experiences of GBV due to mistreatment in the social services system and criminal justice system. When they do report, they often suffer more severe consequences, including having their children removed from the home (Bent-Goodly 2009). When Black survivors of abuse defend themselves, they too are at risk of incarceration. Black women and girls are an overrepresented demographic among those who experience childhood sexual abuse. A recent study by the Human Rights Project found that "sexual abuse is one of the primary predictors of a girl's entry into the juvenile justice system" (Saar et al., 2015). There are more women in U.S. prisons now than ever before in the nation's carceral history. A disproportionate number of these women are Black, Latinx, poor and queer (Young 2016). Black teens often do not recognize GBV in intimate relationships unless it involves physical abuse or rape. A study of African American teens and intimate partner violence revealed "there was more variation in the labeling of other abuse scenarios. Some of the contextual factors that influenced participant designation included the gender and intent of the perpetrator, the impact on the victim, and the role the victim 'played' in the abuse. Participants had more permissive attitudes regarding acts that were interpreted as typical behaviors in dating relationships" (Storer et al., 2019). Black women and girls experience disproportionate amounts of GBV, suffer greater consequences of GBV, and rarely garner justice when they are victims of GBV. This confluence of factors makes it difficult to recognize GBV in the lives of Black women and girls. Officer Casebolt's treatment of Dejerria Becton is informed by his misogynoir and is an example of Gender Based Violence. The inability for consumers of the video to read the McKinney pool party encounter as evidence Gender Based Violence, is an example of mediated misogynoir in a *digital* environment, a phenomenon I call "viral misogynoir."

VIRAL MISOGYNOIR

In *The Suffering Will Not Be Televised*, Rebecca Wanzo traces the invisibility of Black women's suffering in media narratives about social violence and victimization. She claims Black women are excluded from sentimental political storytelling—texts that present events or conflicts in simplistic emotional binaries that are meant to provoke an emotional response. Sentimental narratives often flatten the complexity of traumatic events, erasing intersectional analysis as well as the event's links to racial history. Despite this, sentimental political storytelling is a vehicle which helps to garner mobilization efforts. The failure to produce sentimental political narratives for Black women and girls is an example of misogynoir. Misogynoir prevents Black women and girls from fitting into narratives that generate enough sympathy to prompt mobilization. In my efforts to understand what it means to be Black in

America and the subject of Black pain, wounding, and death imagery, I ana-
lyzed eight viral videos of Black people's encounters with law enforcement
and interviewed a total of 20 Black Baltimore-based artists about their viral
video witnessing practices. One artist, a cisgender lesbian poet, noted,

> These videos with women make me think a lot about rape culture; no one
> believes you—you can have the videos and pictures of the assault and it doesn't
> matter what proof we have. It's all about the White gaze and our system is made
> for their future. Forgetfulness is a function of America. Black women have no
> bond with the systems that protect us.

Her statement recalls the (hashtag) #SayHerName research about racialized
violence against Black women at the hands of the police, published in July
2015 by the African American Policy Forum. The report cites that Black
woman make up 7 percent of the population but 22 percent of the domestic
violence incidents. The report also notes, "when Black women do turn to the
police for support, they often fail to secure safety from their abusive partners.
More disturbingly, an alarming number of police killings of Black women
take place in the context of police response to domestic violence situations"
(22). *Viral misogynoir* is the failure to read and recognize videos of violent
interactions between Black women and police as informed by misogynoir and
evidence of state-sanctioned Gender-Based Violence.

Analysis of viral misogynoir reveals Black women and girls are treated
as something to be feared, not protected. For example, in the footage of the
McKinney Pool Party Incident, Dajerria Becton is unarmed. She is walking
away from Eric Casebolt when Casebolt grabs her by the hair and wrestles
her to the ground. As young people scream and turn to the aid of Becton, a
large, white male resident in a yellow polo shirt and khaki pants thrusts his
hands out to both sides of his body, pushing the children away. Casebolt
retrieves his handgun and points it at several of the young, Black male teenag-
ers attempting to help Becton. While this is occurring, 15-year-old Dajerria is
crying for her mother. After this video went viral, Eric Casebolt was placed
on leave and three years later, Becton won a $148,000 settlement against the
city of McKinney, Texas. In an interview in *Teen Vogue*, Becton's lawyer,
Kim T. Cole, reported that Dajerria hasn't been swimming since the incident
occurred (Richie 2017).

In the video, it is unclear what danger or threat Dajerria Becton posed
for Officer Eric Casebolt. Dajerria seems to be penalized for simply "talking back"—phenomena bell hooks describe as "speaking as an equal to an
authority figure" (2015, 1989). In 2014, researchers found that whites attrib-
uted a super humanization to Blacks whereby Black people are perceived as
having supernatural, extrasensory, and magical mental and physical qualities

(Waytz et al., 2015). Further study links these perceptions to excess cruelty, punishment, and suffering of Black women under the hands of the police. It also links back to the adultification of Black girls, an obvious assertion considering the McKinney pool party incident.

In Diamond Reynolds' viral video of Philando Castile's murder, we see how being *perceived* as monstrous and superhuman mutes the ability to garner empathy and receive fundamental recognition of humanity from the state. Throughout the video, we hear Castile groaning in pain. Diamond Reynolds speaks in a calm and matter-of-fact manner as she addresses Officer Yanez, telling him, "*He is licensed to carry. He was trying to get his wallet and ID out of his pocket, and he wanted to let you know that he had a firearm and was reaching for his wallet.*" While recording the video with a shaky hand, Reynolds simultaneously answers the officer with a measured voice and explains what is happening moment by moment, alternating between addressing her Facebook audience and answering the officer's questions. As Yanez becomes increasingly agitated, screaming, "*Ma'am, keep your hands where they are!*" Reynolds continues to speak in a composed manner, stating, "*I will sir, no worries.*" She then addresses the audience with, "*He just shot his (Castile's) arm off.* " While she is talking, Officer Yanez begins screaming, "*I told him not to reach for it. I told him to get his hand open.*" Reynolds responds, "*You told him to get his ID sir and his driver's license.*" At 1 minute and 32 seconds, Diamond Reynolds realizes her boyfriend is most likely dead, stating, "*Oh my God, please don't tell me he's dead. Please don't tell me my boyfriend just went like that.*' Officer Yanez does not respond to this statement. Diamond Reynolds shakily pans her cell phone camera in the rapid back and forth motions between herself and back to the driver's seat where Philando Castile has expired. These physical motions as captured by her cell phone footage contradict the measured and calm way she continues to address Yanez as the officer barks orders at her and points a gun in her face. As Yanez continues to hold a gun on Reynolds, her four-year-old daughter pleads for her mother to remain calm. '*It's OK, I'm right here with you,*' Reynolds' daughter, Dae'Anna can be heard saying. Later, she adds, '*Mom, please stop cussing and screaming 'cause I don't want you to get shooted.*" At four years old, her daughter comforts her mother while being terrorized and traumatized herself. Despite Reynolds' efforts to be nonthreatening and worthy of empathy, Yanez still forces her out of the car, onto her knees and violently restrains her, intimately entwinning her body in his forceful embrace. His treatment of her body is outsized in proportion to her actions throughout the encounter. All of this occurs as her daughter cries in the background.

The video of Diamond Reynolds and the McKinney pool party incident are just two examples of viral misogynoir to surface within the last several years. In summer 2014, a viral video surfaced of 51-year-old Marlene Pinnock being beaten on the side of the freeway by a California Highway Patrol. The cellular phone video captures this Black woman's pain as she is straddled and repeatedly punched in the head and face by the white patrolman. Pinnock has a history of mental illness and refused to stop walking into traffic. According to the officer, she pushed him. He retaliated by throwing her to the ground and physically assaulting her. During that same year, Arizona State University professor, Ersula Ore was violently arrested for jaywalking on campus. The footage of her arrest was captured via cellular phone and showed the police officer handcuffing and slamming her to the ground, causing her skirt to hike up (Bourdieu 2014). In 2016 in Maryland, police responded to a 911 call involving a 15-year-old girl after she crashed her bike into the side of a car. The girl resisted engaging with the police, and her actions were described as "combative, kicking, cursing and refusing to identify herself." Officers handcuffed, pepper-sprayed her, charged her with assault, disorderly conduct, possession of marijuana, and a traffic violation (Jacobo 2016). On April 22, 2018, a viral video surfaced of three White police officers violently arresting Chikesia Clemons, a 25-year-old Black woman, after an employee of the Waffle House in Saraland, Alabama, called 911. While Clemons explains that she asked the employee for the phone number to corporate headquarters so she could lodge a complaint, an officer grabs Clemons' neck, and wrists. The next scene shows Clemons on the floor as two police officers grab at her body and her clothing, exposing her breasts. The police officers threaten to break her arm while simultaneously choking her. Meanwhile, Clemons repeatedly asks why she is being cuffed. She receives no clear answer. She was later charged with disorderly conduct and resisting arrest (Haag 2018). In 2018, a viral video surfaced of 15-year-old-Jasmine Darwin being body-slammed by Police Officer Ruben De Los Santos at Rolesville High School in Rolesville, North Carolina. The video shows footage of a crowd of students, then the officer picks the girl up over his head and slams her to the ground. He then picked up her limp body, places her in handcuffs, and drags her away (CNN 2018). Also in 2018, a video surfaced of a police officer assaulting a 14-year-old girl in Coral Springs, Florida. In the video, an officer can be seen punching her twice in her side as she lay prone with her face in the dirt, his knee in her back, gripping and yanking her by the hem of her jean shorts. According to Coral Springs police, her treatment was warranted because she "resisted arrest," saying the young teen was "unruly" and part of a group who were allegedly harassing patrons at a mall (CNN 2018). Each story of viral misogynoir involves a Black woman or girl talking back to officers, thus "warranting" their violent, intimate arrest. As Sheri Parks suggests in *Fierce Angels*, "whether it was a gift of the goddess or forged in the suffering of their lives, black women have persevered and practiced a type of female strength that has been true to the lives of women as they lived them, a type of female strength that has kept them and their families alive when everything else was working against them" (206). It is disappointing that Black women's suffering is often only legible in narratives of Black female resilience. We could argue that Diamond Reynolds' measured, calm response to Officer Yanez is an example of her being the quintessential "strong black woman," at the same time, her strength was not armor enough to prevent state violence from catastrophically impacting her life. Her strong black woman status did not win her justice. In fact, it exacerbated the violence against her. These incidents of viral misogynoir exemplify Robin M. Boylorn's suggestion that,

> Society refuses to see Black girls as victims. We are made to believe that our feelings are dangerous, so we suppress them. We are told, repeatedly, even among ourselves, that we are not fragile, so we think we must live up to those expectations. When unthinkable and unspeakable things happen, we take a deep breath, hold back tears, and swallow our sadness. We perform strength like nobody's business. (28)

In the eyes of the state and in the mediated environment, these arrested Black women and girls are either seen as unruly monsters or examples of the superhuman. Viral misogynoir thrives when Black women and girls are denied their complex emotional responses to law enforcement overreach, and thus, are denied their fundamental humanity.

SPREADING VIRAL MISOGYNOIR

Texts that qualify as viral misogynoir generally involve a Black woman or girl who is responding to what Ruth Wilson-Gilmore refers to as, "state terrorism" and who must deal with "the price of misbehavin,' of acting out" (31). Black women and girls' charged responses to white male authority and state terrorism, "have been policed in brutal and deadly ways ever since the formation of slave patrols in the mid-eighteenth century" (Richie 2019). Black women's experiences of racial profiling and police violence are just as prevalent and embedded in the history of the U.S. police force but are often invisible in discourse about prison abolition, mass incarceration and police violence. As school psychologists, Dr. Tawanna Jones Morrison says, "Black girls live in the same homes, attend the same schools and are touched by the same experiences as Black boys but many people do not understand the impact police violence has on the lives of Black women and girls" (Ms. Magazine, 2020). Due to media convergence, viral videos of Black women and girls' encounters with law enforcement spread quickly, garnering intense sharing and commentary from across the media landscape. These videos generate an excess of heat before the flame peters out to be replaced by something more comprehensible in the news cycle. It is as if people are unable to hold issues of sexism and racism (misogynoir) in their collective consciousness simultaneously. I believe this is because media consumers are unable to process narratives that are focused *solely* on the lives of Black women and girls. A race and gender-biased media landscape is one major factor in this.

MEDIA LANDSCAPE

In our society of spectacle and surveillance, much of what we see is controlled by corporate media outlets (Baker 116) with agendas created to maintain the status quo. In her investigation into media, the police, and stories about Black female victims of homicide, sociologist Cheryl L. Neely suggests, "a reporter's willingness to provide a compassionate view of the victim may be directly related to the race of the reporter" (43). A 2018 study by the Pew Research Center found newsroom employees are more likely to be white and male than all U.S. workers. According to the 2018 Status of Women of Color in the U.S. News Media report, women of color represent only, "7.95 percent of U.S. print newsroom staff, 12.6 percent of local TV news staff, and 6.2 percent of local radio staff." The lack of women of color in decision-making roles in U.S. newsrooms contributes to mispresentations of women, sexist coverage of policies that impact Black women's lives, and underrepresentation of stories essential to the health and safety of Black women and girls in the U.S. In this biased news landscape, "the act of determining which victims are salient enough for media attention essentially entrenches the belief that some victims have less value" (Neely, 2015, 46). In the news, if Black men are overrepresented as assailants and white women are represented as the only victims, the reality of gender-based violence against Black women and girls is illegible.

A 2020 article in *Glamour Magazine* focused on the experiences and responsibility that comes with being a Black female journalist. The eight reporters interviewed all shared how exhausting it can be to report on issues of racially disproportionate police brutality while being a member of the group that is being brutalized. Journalist Stacie-Marie Ishmael, Editing Director of the *Texas Tribune* says, "there is a notion that certain kinds of experiences disqualify you from being able to objectively assess a situation. And I have found that the kinds of experiences that ostensibly disqualify you are rooted in things that make you different from the status quo in most newsrooms" (5). Her statement provides insight into the complicated relationship Black female newsgatherers have when reporting on stories about Black women and girls. The notion of "objective journalism" makes the claim that there is some default, neutral party reporting on events. This default neutral often represents the make-up of the white, male-dominated newsroom where it is enforced. Black female journalist must deal with the constant dismissal of their expertise in the structuring of these news stories. Additionally, many of the journalists report having a responsibility to help Black viewers understand how to read viral images and respond when being interviewed. Black female reporters have the Herculean task of providing context, educating the public, shaping the narrative, and surviving Black oppression in newsrooms that are disproportionately white and male.

Black-owned newspapers are often owned and operated by Black women but that does not mean they create environments where Black women are safe. In summer of 2020 *Essence* magazine experienced intense scrutiny after a group of former employees under the name #BlackFemaleAnonymous, penned a letter in *Medium* criticizing the company's treatment of Black women. Their letter not only levels multiple indictments about an allegedly toxic culture at Essence Ventures, but it also demands the resignation of several key members of leadership. It also calls for the brand's key sponsors— which include AT&T, Coca Cola, Chase Bank, Ford, McDonald's, Procter & Gamble, Walmart, and Warner Media—to divest until there is new leadership in place. A magazine that caters to the uplift of Black women created a hostile environment for Black women. This raises doubts about the magazine's ability to provide authentic coverage of Black female experiences, especially experiences of poor Black women.

Black female television anchors continue to experience ill treatment in network and cable news outlets. In 2016, scholar Melissa Harris-Perry departed from MSNBC alleging that they tried to silence her from providing her customary intersectional analysis during an election year. In 2017, Tamron Hall abruptly left NBC's *Today Show* after her nine am slot was given to former Fox News anchor Megan Kelly. These high-profile tensions between prominent Black female news anchors and major media corporations present an environment that seems largely toxic to Black female approaches to storytelling.

Black women also only make up a fraction of highly paid and prominent film and television creators. USC Annenberg's 2020 Inclusion Initiative Report found that male directors still outnumber female directors 20 to 1, and that Hollywood's perception of a female director is a white woman. Additionally, "only 13 women from underrepresented racial/ethnic groups have directed any of the 1,300 top movies from 2007 to 2019. This is less than 1% of all directing jobs (n=1,448) whereas white males held 82.5% of jobs, underrepresented males 12.6% of jobs, and white females 3.9% of jobs (2)." Black female journalists are not able to frame the news in ways that illuminate the complex intersections that make up their existence and Black female movie-makers are rarely provided avenues to imagine the complexity of Black women and girls' experiences on screen. Combined, this leaves media consumers with very little material to understand Black women and girl's responses and actions in viral misogynoir texts.

BLACK WOMEN AND GIRLS IN THE CULTURAL IMAGINATION

Sociologist Patricia Hill Collins developed the concept of controlling images to describe the containers media have used to shape Black women's existence. Linking the controlling images of mammies, matriarchs, sapphires, jezebels, and welfare-queens to Black women's ability to establish economic and political power, Collins provides a potent analytic in efforts to understand media culture's impact on Black women and girls. Controlling images have been essential to the political economy of domination fostering Black women's oppression (Collins 2005). For example, if a Black woman in the workplace is afraid of being seen as dominating and angry (traits essential to the controlling image of the sapphire), that Black woman may not advocate for her well-being in the workplace when it becomes necessary. At the root of controlling images is the perception of Black women's hypersexuality or asexuality. Controlling images attach themselves to Black women and girls regardless of their class, education, or achievement (Snider 2018).

Essential to controlling images is a process of projection. In psychological terms, this is the act of projecting undesirable feelings and emotions onto someone else. This term, first coined by Sigmund Freud in 1894, was initially believed to be a defense against acknowledging undesirable aspects in oneself (Salem Press 2019). Over the years, the theory has also broadened to help explain theories of the self, in-group, and out-group identity, as well as one's expectations about their future selves (D'Argembeau 2012). Black women and girls are constantly projected upon by a myriad of forces within and outside of Black communities. As the ultimate abject other, Black women and girls' bodies are frequently positioned in relation to whites, Black men, and other Black women (Zachery 2017). In *But Some of Us Are Brave* (1982), Gloria T. Hull and Barbara Smith wrote,

> Because of white women's racism and Black men's sexism, there was no room in either area [women's liberation or Black Power] for a serious consideration of the lives of Black women. And even when they have considered Black women, white women usually have not had the capacity to analyze racial politics and Black culture, and Black men have remained blind or resistant to the implications of sexual politics in Black women's lives. (xxi)

Viral misogynoir illustrates how these sentiments still ring true almost forty years later. This positioning of Black women and girls as outside of women's liberation and Black civil rights, opens Black women and girls up to three key relational scripts. These scripts allow viral misogynoir to thrive.

Script 1: Black Liberation Is Black *Male* Liberation

Narratives of Black freedom are often patriarchal in nature because Black is often synonymous with male. This comes out in Black liberation ethos which often rely on patriarchal hierarchies. Black male exceptionalism programs are a perfect example of this problematic discourse. When Black men are positioned as an "endangered species" on the social index, programs are created which invisiblize the struggles of Black women. Recent studies have illustrated race gaps in intergenerational mobility largely reflect the poor outcomes for black men (Chetty, Hendren, Jones, Porter 2018). However, there is a lack of empirical data to support the overall claim that Black males are more burdened by inequalities than Black females. Exploring meta-text found in Black male exceptionalism interventions, Paul Butler says these programs suggests,

> Fixing Black male problems is a way to establish racial justice. Another is that African American women bear some responsibility for the subordination of African American men. A third is that Black male problems are more deserving of remedies than Black female problems. A fourth is that racism, discrimination, and White supremacy have affected Black men more adversely than Black women [and] . . . African American masculinity should be championed as a matter of public policy. (2013)

These tenants illuminate patriarchal hierarchies of thinking. Assistant Secretary of Labor, Patrick Moynihan's 1965 report, "The Negro Family, The Case for National Action" positioned Black women as emasculating figures responsible for reproducing degenerate children. His report went on to suggest the solution to Black poverty rests on bringing supposedly absent fathers back into Black households to restore patriarchal domestic configurations. As many scholars have noted, this report effectively scapegoat's Black women as the vessel for Black disenfranchisement. In doing so, it obscures the actual institutional and structural racial inequalities embedded in American systems of government. Moynihan's report as well as the Welfare reform and Urban Renewal policies that followed its publication, successfully projected a host of problematics onto Black women and girls' bodies.

Further in his investigation, Butler highlights how Black male exceptionalism advocacy often supports, "African American women when, or because, the interventions will benefit African American men" (489). This is not a new approach to Black liberation. In *The Narrative of Frederick Douglass*, the abolitionist comes to understand the horrors of slavery only by witnessing the merciless abuse of his Aunt Hester at the hands of their master, Captain Anthony. Douglass' realization hinges upon his own feelings of vulnerability, not his empathy for Aunt Hester's particular positionality on that plantation. In 1962, Malcolm X is famously quoted as saying the "most disrespected person in America is the black woman. The most unprotected person in America is the black woman. The most neglected person in America is the Black woman" (1962). He goes on to suggest that Black men must be willing to lay down their lives to protect and support "our" women. As liberatory as this statement is, it remains steeped in patriarchy. In her investigation of patri-archal structures within the Nation of Islam (NOI), Ula Y. Taylor describes Black female NOI members as inhabiting a slippery slope between being seen as one deserving of loving protection and being deemed one's property (2017, 175). These women were and are enamored with the idea of a system that promises protection, financial stability, and a repudiation of the devalua-tion of Black womanhood. Yet, for this liberatory state to exist, Black women in NOI must abdicate some parts of their self-determination. In the Black civil rights movements from the '20s through the '60s, Black women such as Ida B. Wells, Fannie Lou Hammer and countless female leaders on the local level were essential to the organizing and mobilization of those efforts. In *The Dark Side of the Street: Black Women, Rape and Resistance, A New History of the Civil Rights Movement from Rosa Parks to Black Power*, Danielle McGuire shows how the early Gender-Based Violence advocacy work of NAACP leaders such as Rosa Parks helped lay the groundwork for the Black civil rights movements of the fifties. Yet, Black women are rarely held up as the icons of those movements the way Black male leaders have come to be seen. In fact, the rampant sexual abuse and brutality Black female civil rights activists experienced at the hands of the police, "garnered neither the media coverage nor the organizational support necessary to stop them from happen-ing" (46). This is in large part due to a historical silencing of Black women's responses to sexual violence. As Patricia Broussard says,

> The clear message to Black women has been to shut up and suffer in silence. Likewise, Black women's silence has empowered White men because in the past, Black women have feared repercussions against them and those they love. This knowledge, coupled with the lack of laws protecting Black women, empowered White men to continue the physical and sexual abuse of Black women for centuries. (2013)

That fact that movements to end sexual violence are rarely an agenda in Black civil rights movements, illuminates the inability to give racism and sexism equal weight in social justice arenas. The modern movement for Black Lives was founded by Black, queer women who advocate for lives of all Black and brown men, women, and gender-nonconforming victims impacted by police brutality, yet the names of women and gender-nonconforming victims are not sustained in the cultural imaginary. Equating Black empowerment with justice for Black men, makes Black women worthy *only* in relation to Black men.

Script 2: Black Women and Girls Are Avatars

A thread undergirding muted mobilizations for Black women and girls is the tendency to position them as symbolic figures. Symbolism is the process of one thing representing another (Firth 2011). Often that which stands for something inhabits an outsized weight, and "Black leaders attempting to rearticulate the meaning of black in American society have time after time used the black woman as symbolic material" (Craig 2002). Throughout the years, Black representations of Black women have been used rhetorically to signal racial progress or racial degeneracy. A 1966 issues of Ebony magazine asks, "Are Negro Girls Getting Prettier?." On the cover are five lighter-skinned Black women with straightened hair and thin noses. Within the article, medical doctors and health experts point to better nutrition, grooming and other enhancements, noting Black women no longer have, "the spindly legs, sagging bosoms, unruly rumps and ungroomed heads that marred many a protentional lovely of yesteryear" (25). Ebony magazine has been a staple in Black American life for decades. Articles such as this highlight the tendency to 1) equate Black racial progress with proximity to White standards; and 2) to see and use the Black female body as a vessel with which to gauge Black progress. There was a fierce backlash against this article when it appeared, with Black readers pointing out that, "We've been pretty all along" and calling to question the magazine's decision to only feature lighter skinned Black women as beautiful. Yet, Black women have not been merely pawns in this discourse. According to Maxine Craig,

> They actively participated in the process of reinventing the image of the race through their words and conduct. In speeches and writing, female leaders chose from and reshaped the culturally available images of womanhood. Ordinary black women participated in racial re-articulation in their day-to-day lives by positioning themselves in relation to an ever-changing world of representation. (129)

Craig's assessment highlights the primacy of the visual in political rhetoric about racial progress. Representation matters and the Black female body has always been used to challenge racial hierarchies while also putting Black women and girls in their place within a patriarchal system. As Margo Jefferson contends, "the burden of being a constant symbol, of having to live up to a symbol of advancement, of progress, of being perfect in some way and always representing the destiny of an entire people—that is supposed to be invincibility. That's enormous" (2015). In her investigation of the way scripts are inscribed upon Black female bodies, Jordan-Zachary suggests, "scripting is understood as the process of the transformation of the body into discursive text, to which signs and stereotypes can then be applied for the purpose of assigning meaning" (32). Some of the scripts inscribed upon black women and girls are: Strong Black Woman (Zachary 2017), Hypersexual Other (Collins 1991), Superwoman (Wallace 1979), and Welfare Queen (Collins 2005). These scripts position Black women and girls as mute and abject caretakers of degenerate brood, or loud, excessive, and uncontrollable. Sharon Patricia Holland says Black women, "are so malleable, so brilliantly represented as a constant within our stubborn inconsistency that we can be manipulated while remaining simultaneously resistant to all attempts at regulation. At our most dangerous moment black women serve the nation even more adequately as the instigators of black men's demise" (18). Weighted down by these scripts, when Black women and girls are positioned as symbolic figures in a mediated space, they effectively become avatars.

In the language of game studies, an avatar is, "a computer-generated figure controlled by a person via a computer" (Coleman 2011). The player is generally able to operate the avatar in as close to "real time" as possible, creating a synchronous experience for the user. In a videogame, the "avatar does not independently move and feel but is the means through which the player's movement and feeling is expressed within the game environment and the events unfolding within that virtual world" (Owen 2017). The player completes actions in the game world that impact the player's experiences in the real life, creating a feedback loop between the player and the avatar. Outside of the world of game studies, the concept of the avatar has taken on even richer meaning. In *Avatar Bodies*, Ann Weinstone proposes that when we stop ordering the other to be other—whether technological, animal, or simply inanimate, we become avatar bodies, consisting of shared gestures, skills, memories, sensations, beliefs, and affects. She suggests, "within this zone of relationality, the categories of self and other are rendered undecidable, are suspended but not dismissed, and the ontogenic touch of other people is proffered under the sign of pleasure" (41). Avatar bodies are absorbing and permeable, allowing a shared sense of connection that, if practiced thoughtfully, has the means to create a better, more solidly relational world. But the concept of the permeability and absorption of the other is complicated territory when applied to diasporic Black people, whose bodies have often been treated as disembodied objects.

In *Embodied Avatars: Genealogies of Black Feminist Art and Performance*, Uri McMillan uses the term avatar to describe the way Black women become "simulated beings" to perform objecthood, "an adroit method of circumventing prescribed limitations on black women in the public sphere while staging art and alterity in unforeseen places" (7). As avatars, these women practice a deliberate self-objectification to aid in their liberation and call to question projections placed upon the female Black body. By doing so, they disrupt our understanding of objectified bodies and embodied subjectivity. McMillan's investigation is useful in that it negates the immediate assumption that to become a Black object is to be stripped of agency and subjective experience. However, McMillan's investigation explores this elasticity within the context of formal and informal performance art which points to the avatar's awareness of the existence of an audience, as well as a deliberate act of personal signification. Black women and girls swept up in the tide of viral misogynoir rarely have a say in who and how people get to witness their encounters. Other than Diamond Reynolds' use of her cellular phone in the death of Philando Castile, most Black women and girls have no control over how their avatars travel in a digital landscape.

The permeability of avatar bodies as a positive development conflict with the notion of Black embodiment, and the creation of the black body. Scholars of Black life have grappled with embodiment over the years. Harvey Young suggests the "*idea* of the black body has been and continues to be projected across actual physical bodies" (4) resulting in misrecognition of individuated Black people. Young goes on to claim, "when popular connotations of blackness are mapped across or internalized within black people, the result is the creation of the *black body* [author emphasis] an abstract figure which "shadows or doubles the real one" (5). It may be the "shadow Black body" that is violently restrained for trespassing when attending a pool party, but it is an actual Black teenage girl who must deal with the material and traumatic consequences of Gender Based Violence at the hands of a state agent. These projections of blackness structure embodied Black experiences across generations and continents. Because of diasporic anti-blackness, one individual Black body can stand for the whole of Black bodies.

To frame Black women and girls as avatars in viral misogynoir, it is necessary to meld notions of the embodied Black experience with game theories understanding of an avatar as a figure controlled by a user. A key component coupling the two is the concept of liveness. In game studies, internet liveness, digital liveness and virtual liveness all speak to a false sense of community and connection, despite not being in physical proximity. In media studies, liveness refers to both the temporal nature i.e., experiencing something as it is happening, and the spatial structure i.e., being in the location where something is happening. Some mediums lend themselves more to liveness than others. For example, television news represents liveness while a narrative film or documentary does not. Usually, "watching something live" means "watching as it is being filmed." Nothing is "live" unless you are there to witness it occurring. Discussing television depictions of African Americans over the years, Sasha Torres suggests that American television has always had "a certain documentary or ethnographic impulse, an imperative to 'authenticity' in depictions of African Americans" (Torres 2003, 13). Television programming such as *Cops* have certainly helped fuel this quest for live, realistic depictions of Black monstrosity, as has footage of mass protests racist injustice such as those in Baltimore following the death of Freddie Gray Jr. This impulse to document Black bodies, especially female ones, occurs in both digital and performance environments. A good example of this is Ayanna Evan's "Operation Catsuit" which was performed at MoMa in early 2020. As a performance artist, Evans donned a neon green tiger printed catsuit and walked the streets of New York to the museum. During her walk and even at the museum, patrons snapped pictures of her body—though all she was doing was existing in her own flesh. As Black women are often seen as excessive in body, mind and spirit, the performance provided Evan's plenty of material to critique the ethnographic impulses that comes with being an avatar. Viral videos operate like "live" news programming but travel like liveness in game studies. Viral videos of Black pain, wounding and death contain spectacular violence, are endlessly repeated, and often roped into cycles of impression management (sharing, responding, shaping discourse). This type of impression management mimics the false sense of community and connection found in game studies. As such, viral videos are a new form of media liveness which help create Black female avatar bodies.

Viral misogynoir hinges on seeing the bodies of Black women and girls as a symbolic mass that can be embodied by others in the digital environment. Their pain can be used to make a point about other people's plights, without necessarily benefiting Black women and girls. The technology might be new, but the phenomena is not. In the 1980s, Black women writers helped birth a wave of sexual abuse trauma narratives, including Toni Morrison's *The Bluest Eye*, Maya Angelou's *I Know Why the Caged Bird Sings* and Alice Walker's *The Color Purple.* Each of these texts grappled with sexual violence, race, identity, and class, and helped to advance the second wave feminist sexual abuse advocacy movement dedicated to "breaking the silence." Trauma survivor narratives in this era successfully advanced anti-sexual violence advocacy efforts. These narratives were designed to change systems from a collective cultural standpoint and make real Judith Herman's concept of "remembering and telling the truth about horrible events" to create spaces of healing (36). Feminist advocacy against rape (politics), bolstered by Black Women's narratives of sexual trauma (data) helped increase crime control measures reinforced by the neoliberal turn to the state as the enforcer of "normal" family values. Put simply, "governmental apparatuses tend to use statistics about violence against women of color to ground legislation fundamentally oriented to protecting white women" (Harkins). By reading Black women narratives, white feminists were able to embody Black women and Black girlhood to create policies that furthered their own liberation, while erasing the racialized materiality of Black women and girls' Gender-Based Violence.

Script 3: Misrecognition Through Visual Rhetoric

To be Black is to inhabit an ongoing state of becoming. What counts as authentic Blackness changes over time and in relation to social, cultural, and political shifts. A global Black diaspora links Black people in America to Black people around the world through a shared legacy of oppression and revolution (Gilroy 1993), further broadening what it means to embody a Black experience. The constant construction and deconstruction of what it means to be Black is the thing that makes "Black culture" (Johnson 2003). Blackness is contingent upon the way it circulates visually. The visual determines how people think about one another and how they think about themselves. Visual rhetoric argues images, especially photographs and other physical artifacts apart from the written word, are powerful symbols for developing and negotiating meanings in society (DiBari Jr., Samson 2018). Our society of spectacle and surveillance hinges on the primacy of all things visual, so, to understand how viral misogynoir works, it is important to also understand how Black bodies are seen.

Building off Judith Butler's contention that the visual field can never be neutral to race, George Yancy describes the white gaze as "a racist socio-epistemic aperture" (14). It is a way of seeing that creates and is created by a racist reality. This way of seeing teaches viewers to associate Black bodies with violence and white bodies with purity. By positioning Black people as abject figures, white people can see themselves as the norm—as unraced, default beings of innocence. This positioning is supported and co-constituted in every societal structure, as is evidenced by diasporic anti-Blackness. Unpacking the dashcam footage of the violent arrest of Sandra Bland by Officer Encina, Yancy states, "it's not about what the Black body does, but about what the white gaze sees, what it constructs" (252). Because a vast majority of white people do not see themselves as racialized, they fail to see the historical contexts undergirding their actions. With this perspective it becomes impossible for them to see what Black people see when they encounter white people in positions of authority. Encounters between Black women and girls and state authority escalate due to the misogynoir(esq) meta-narratives white officers refuse to acknowledge. That violent spectacle is captured on video, becoming viral misogynoir. How and what we see when looking at viral misogynoir is determined by cultural conventions and the meta-narratives which support them. What is seen is overdetermined by a racial scopic regime (Lebduski 2014) which relies on this binary between normal and abject. Black women and girls are not only positioned as abject because they are Black; they are also dubbed abject because of their per-ceived gender-related aberrance.

Viral misogynoir is a unique type of visual rhetoric that communicates very specific, often distorted messages about the availability and excesses of Black women and girls' bodies. In *Troubling Vision: Performance, Visuality and Blackness*, Nicole Fleetwood argues, "the black female body is always already troubling to the dominant visual culture" (113). Fleetwood links this troubling to the concept of excess flesh enactments, a scopic method of look-ing designed to discipline the Black female body by positioning it as being too much. She argues, "the black visual has been framed as masculine, which has positioned the black female visual as excess" (253). Black female bodies trouble, "dominant public culture and . . . black masculinist debates about race, subjectivity, and visuality" (252). The Black female body is often *only* legible when it is positioned as accessible, available, and sexually deviant (hooks 1992, 2015). These misogynoir(esq) meta-narratives about Black women and girls are rarely acknowledged but always acted upon.

Viral misogynoir is a discourse about seeing and being seen. These texts do not just circulate because of their spectacular violence. They also travel because sharers believe that visual testimony to injustice will somehow gar-ner justice. This liberation tactic is not new. Sadiya Hartman traces it back to abolitionist practices in the nineteenth century and the endless circulation of images of enslaved Black people in various states of pain, wounding, and death. In the attempt to garner empathy for enslaved Black people, aboli-tionists sought to "bring suffering nearer" (18) to foster sentimentality. She argues, "empathy is a projection of oneself into another in order to better understand the other" (19). There is a danger to this type of affective agency (Wanzo 2009), especially when Black female bodies are always seen as open for the taking on. Viral misogynoir exists within a history of visual rhetoric used to call out and shame those who commit or allow atrocities to occur. The success of naming and shaming rests on calling attention to the failure of weak institutions and shaming the wider public that does not challenge the status quo (Lawrence, Roberts 2019). Viral misogynoir relies on pathos to mobilize sentiment, yet it rarely attaches itself to a specific action. Pathos pulls at heart strings—ethos pulls at shared sense of community and asks that we identify with the victim.

Viral misogynoir does not foment the level of pathos and ethos needed to thwart the racist socio-epistemic aperture. These violent, spectacular images live on in perpetuity, garnering muted justice. Much of this has to do with the nature of the racist and sexist digital landscape in which it travels.

VIRAL MISOGYNOIR AND DIGITAL ACTIVISM

The world of viral misogynoir relies not only on viral videos but also the hashtags, memes, and visual rhetoric which reinforce its messaging. To go viral, a text must circulate heavily, and go through a process of transformation that reflect, amplifies, and distorts it. Critical in viral misogynoir is this aspect of distortion. If Black bodies already trouble the dominant visual field, the distorted aspect of the digital environment creates a recipe for visual misrecognition. As An Xiao Mina points out, "just because people are paying attention and hearing the narratives. . . doesn't mean they come to the same conclusions" (213). The viral digital environment is a participatory ecosystem with divergent actors holding multiple, sometimes obscure agendas. In this environment, historic misrepresentations collide with viral videos, hashtags, and memes about unruly, loud and "ghetto" Black women and girls. The digital environment reflects the culture and systems that have created it—as such, the internet has its own racist socio-epistemic aperture. In *Digitizing Race: Visual Cultures of the Internet*, Lisa Nakumura explains the internet,

> is a visual technology, a protocol for seeing that is interfaced and networked in ways that produce a particular set of racial formations. These formations arose in a specific historical period: the premillennial neoliberal moment when race was disappeared from public and governmental discourse while at the same time policies regarding Internet infrastructures and access were being formed. (3)

The internet is structured by a combination of visuality and erasure, mimicking the globalized world in which it was born. For many, globalization was responsible for "destroying stable localities, displacing people, and bringing [in] a market-driven branded 'homogenization' of cultural experiences" (Tomilson 1999). This is of course a narrow understanding of identity as something fragile and sovereign, not a process that is shaped by external forces. The Web 2.0 environment of yesteryear prided itself as a digital utopian third space where "identities" could be reshaped, eschewed, or created. Web 2.0. was theoretically a place where users had infinite access to information and like-minded communities This digital utopia was positioned as the great equalizer. The internet remains a "site for identity construction and community formation around racial and ethnic identity" (Daniels 2012). But, as many scholars of digital studies and race have critiqued over the years, there can be no equalizer when the structures of inequity are baked into every system—even newly formed ones.

The internet thrives because of media convergence that privileges the visual over the textual. Ongoing debates about the impact of technology on critical thinking reveal, "large segments of audience are exaggerating their awareness of political issues and do not realize that their online behavior is driven more by emotions than by critical assessment of primary sources" (Plencer 2014). Additionally, following the 2016 presidential election of Donald Trump, researchers found that 62 percent of Americans received their news from social media (Gottfried and Shearer 2016) where millions spread disinformation about the candidates (Allcott and Gentzkow 2017). All evidence points to the fact that the internet has forced users to privilege their ability to code and decode visual rhetoric so much so that "looking has become as important as reading" (Nakumara 2007). The visual culture of the internet complicates "race and racism in new ways" such as the creation of viral content, memes, and hashtags, as well as the increased democratization of media makers. However, these newer visual linguistic tools cannot be separated from the colonial logics that undergird all cultural artifacts.

Discussing how search engines reinforce racism, Safiya Noble says these databases, "oversimplify complex phenomena [and] obscure any struggle over understanding" (Noble 2018). Noble's investigation highlights the way flawed colonial logics of neutrality and objectiveness allows the internet to claim it is neutral to race while being explicitly racist. When a technology becomes commonplace, such as the Google search functions, it often comes to be seen as benign—thus neutral of politics. Her research highlights "algorithmically driven data failures that are specific to people of color and women and to underscore the structural ways that racism and sexism are fundamental to. . . algorithmic oppression" (4). Search engines reflect the damaging hegemonic culture in which they are constructed, but Noble also reminds us that companies like Google exist within a commercial environment where the company's business interests shape what can be found. Her research is a reminder that there is never a neutral position on race when capitalism is at play. Race and capitalism are co-constitutive and wholly dependent on the use of slavery, violence, imperialism, and genocide for profit (Robinson 1983).

For the last decade, the internet has become an increasingly divisive environment, where there is constant "political struggle[s] over racial meaning, knowledge and values (Daniels 2009). This is evidenced by the legitimizing of white supremacist groups who are now referred to as the "alt-right" by the media. It is a term created by online white supremacist groups to distance themselves from their legacy of terrorism associated with Nazism, Fascism, and the Klu Klux Klan. Additionally, while investigating news stories about 4 shooting deaths involving Black people and the police, researchers found out of 1,840 online comments, "profanity or name-calling, were more frequent than deliberative attributes, such as using evidence to support one's point" (Musullo, Fadnis, Whipple 2020). This finding illustrates how hard it is to have meaningful discussions about race and racism in the digital realm. If, as Lisa Nakumura argues, the color-blind discourse of neoliberalism hid the structural racism inherent in its creation, the claim that "concepts that once may have seemed to be an agreed-upon cultural value, such as 'racial equality' or 'diversity,' are now fought over online in ways previously unimagined" (Daniels 2012) is not that unimaginable. Viral misogynoir texts work similarly to Noble's algorithmic oppression. They oversimplify complex meta-narratives and obscure our understanding of them. The explicitly racist comments online suggest that the internet allows for the acting out of what Sharpe calls "nonconsensual racial fantasies" (Sharpe, 1999: 1094). The relative "anonymity" as false as it is considering doxing, still allows people to derail important discourse and spread disinformation. The notion that Black women and girls will receive sustained justice through the sharing of spectacular violence and distorted visual rhetoric is ill-conceived. The digital racist scopic regime is inflexible, no matter how the images are being used. Investigations into cyber activism for Black women and girls reveal even allies have the difficulty in allowing Black women and girls' specific grievances to be heard and acted upon in digital environments.

Researching the effectiveness of the #YesAllWomen campaign that began on Twitter after Elliot Rodger's misogynistic killing spree in 2014, Sarah J. Jackson and Sonia Banaszczyk found that though the campaign helped mainstream the concepts of rape culture and toxic masculinity, none of the discourse "addressed issues of intersectionality or highlighted the explicit standpoints of women who experience multiple axes of oppression" (2016). The participation of women who shared stories of their encounters with rape culture and toxic masculinity were overwhelmingly white. When #YesAllWhiteWomen began to trend in response to this, those critiquing were met with outraged pushback, even though discourse about the exclusion of women of color from mainstream feminist discussions is not a new phenomenon. The warping of the concept of identity politics set forth by the Combahee River Collective (CBC) Statement in 1974 is a perfect example. In a recent *New Yorker* article, scholar Keenga Yamata Taylor interviews founding CBC member Barbara Smith. As Taylor questions Smith about the misuse of the term identity politics, Smith clarifies that identity politics "meant simply this: we have a right as Black women in the nineteen-seventies to formulate our own political agendas" (Smith 2020). Forty-four years later, with a technology CBC member did not know would come to be, the same misrecognition of Black women's advocacy desires remains. When women of color articulated their specific intersectional standpoints using #YesAllWhiteWomen, they were greeted with accusations of toxicity. This is an ongoing trend in feminist discourse where claims of the necessity of a uniform narrative of women's experiences override the experiences of those who have specific positionalities counter to white, cisgender women. Exploring trends in #hashtag feminism, Roopia Risam found that "discourses marked as 'toxic' instantiate gendered and racial notions of online feminism" (2). The tendency to equate intersectional analysis with creating a toxic environment for feminist discourse illustrates the limits of digital environments as a place for advocacy for Black women and girls. Though the digital environment is a place for mainstreaming theory and articulating positionalities, it can never be a neutral or benign space because it is maintained by humans who bring their material conditions with them into the digital realm. Risam goes on to note,

> [white feminists] position women of color as the repository of failure for online feminism, guilty of creating spaces in which white feminists claim a reluctance to speak, for fear of censure. As a result, engagement with intersectional, rather than single-issue, feminism is rendered a problem, a disruption, perhaps even a distraction from the putatively more productive work of an online feminism untroubled by 'infighting' over racial dynamics. (6)

Risam's critique is a reminder that the digital realm is a colonial space and no matter how many counter publics are created in that space, it is still designed to uplift those closer to hegemonic power. In this case, that is white feminists. Even calls for racial justice from Black women suffer in the digital realm. Calling upon Audre Lorde's classic query, "can the masters tools really dismantle the master's house?" geographer Armound Towns critiques the #SayHerName campaign. Town's questions are extremely important to determining the efficacy of viral misogynoir text,

> if one is an activist using communication technologies largely owned by White men (interested in maintaining connections to Western countries) then is one's activism maintaining or challenging global White supremacy? At what point, if any, is the radicalism of #SayHerName consumed whole by the Western control of media technologies? (124)

Town's query sums up the complications of campaigns organized around viral misogynoir-ic text. Overshadowing it all are the linguistic moves of internet content—that can only travel when it is remixed and reimagined.

THE DANGER OF THE REMIX

The internet serves many purposes in our lives. It is a place for building community, activating cultural identity markers, education, engaging in activism, consuming goods, and conducting research. It is also a site of play that allows users the ability to deploy multiple linguistic moves. A move is thought of as a "semantic unit of text that is linked to the writer's purpose" (Amnual 2019). Memes, hashtags, and viral content contribute to the recreational pleasure and enjoyment people experience when in the digital realm. Memes travel well because they can easily be personalized and shared repeatedly. In *Memes to Movements: How the World's Most Viral Media is Changing Social Protests and Power*, An Xiao Mina suggests, "it is in the playful aspects of meme culture that movement narratives can be found" (95). There are image heavy memes, text memes, physical memes, video memes, performative memes, and selfie memes. No matter what kind of meme, each contains some aspect of play designed to evoke feelings. Play, just like education, helps people develop new theories of the world. When people deploy memes to make political or activist statements, their memes take on a life that sometimes maintains the integrity of original but can also become distorted and far removed from the original intent. Their easily shareable nature also provides avenues for the dissemination of false information (Wells 2018). I liken memes to a complex game of telephone that we are playing globally. Mina continues, "memes allow us to more quickly develop the visual and verbal language around which movements organize" (94), even if #hastags and memes are dismissed as slacktivism due to their playful qualities. Hashtags do one of four things: emphasize (calling attention to matters), critique, identify (refer to the author of the post), iterate (express humor) or rally (Daer and Hoffman 2014). Sometimes less playful than visual memes, hashtags also attempt to say a lot with very little, while also provoking feeling in the viewer. The dismissal of memes and hashtags as slacktivism often masks the fact that those who make memes and hashtags for social justice are provoked or activated by something which inspired them to make this specific linguistic move—to articulate a feeling that urgently needed to be put out in the world. Memes, viral videos, and hashtags can be considered affective digital activism. Hashtag activism for the livelihood of Black women and girls can be thought of as a counter-politics, allowing a myriad of types of Black women, girls and femmes, avenues to shape national political conversations about their lives (Jackson 2016). Again, like the game of meme telephone, more legitimized sources of information such as newspapers and academic spaces, often drown out and invisiblize the hashtag activists who create them. #MeToo (Garcia 2017) and #BlackGirlMagic (Thomas 2016) are prime examples of this phenomena. Hashtags and memes allow organizers to shape narratives and drive attention to grievances. If understood as a *part* of a larger strategy for change that has a history of academic and activist work, memes and hashtags literally help sustain movements. Unfortunately, they exist within a digital environment that is shaped by white supremacy, misogyny and the surveillance capitalism which shows up as impression management. These three units contribute to the muted justice efforts and distortions that occur when Black women and girls are victims of state violence and affective digital activism is used to garner justice for them.

Digital campaigns that have been created in the wake March 2020 shooting death of Breonna Taylor by law officers serving a non-knock warrant provide a timely case study of viral distortion inherent to viral misogynoir. Taylor's death as well as the killing of jogger Ahmaud Arbery by white vigilantes in Georgia, and the murder of George Floyd in Minnesota by police officers, has helped elevate the national movement for racial justice and police abolition. Digital activism has been used to elevate the on the ground protests and policy advocacy. In the case of Breonna Taylor, the central demand has been to arrest the police officers who killed her. Throughout the month of May and June, calls for the officer's arrests trended with the straightforward #JusticeforBreonnaTaylor. In July 2020, this online campaign took on a much more satirical linguistic move. As Mary Louise Kelly sums up in a July NPR interview with film and culture critic, Cate Young,

> The central demand, arrest the cops who killed Breonna Taylor. . . [has] gone from a rallying cry to a punchline on social media. It appears in a comedian's tweet about the TV show 'Friends.' It's the caption to a graphic about houseplants. There are self-care posts reminding you to drink plenty of water, wash your hands and arrest the cops who killed Breonna Taylor. (NPR 2020)

These memes set the reader up by beginning with an innocent or unrelated missive and ends with the call for justice to keep the campaign on the top of the media saturation pile. Cate Young suggests this linguistic move both elevates the ask while simultaneously trivializing her death. Young continues,

> But I think that whether or not they are effective for a small segment of the population should not override the fact that it is a disrespectful way to engage with her memory. I think there are lots of things that could be effective. It doesn't necessarily mean that they are the best option. And if there are better options, then they should be taken. I mean, even this phrase, arrest the cops who killed Breonna Taylor, who exactly is that for? Because the rest of us on social media don't have the power to make that happen. We can't actually do the arresting. So, who specifically are you talking to? (3)

Young's questions are central to the debate about the power of viral misogynoir texts, memes, and hashtags. She highlights the ways these linguistic moves make asks that are often impossible for the average media consumers to ensure occur. The movement for police and prison abolition is multilayered and could never contingent upon advocacy around one case or person. The question of respecting Breonna Taylor's memory is even more important in the debates around the effectiveness of these linguistic moves. The remixed call to arrest Breonna Taylor's killers have been used on photoshopped images of L. L. Cool J emerging shirtless from a pool and plastered upon singer Rihanna's backside. Other social media users have used them to promote their brand. A *Bitch* magazine article by Mary Retta highlights other important aspects of this case as it relates to the world of viral misogynoir. She muses, "memes about Taylor are particularly disappointing given how the genre has failed Black women for years. Memes and gifs have long been an avenue for non-Black people on the internet to use digital Blackface" (Retta 2020). Digital blackface describes types of minstrel performance that become available in the digital realm, from using gifs of Black women to show confusion to the repurposing of videos that feature Black people relaying traumatic events in their lives. The "Ain't Nobody Got Time for That" jingle created from Kimberly "Sweet Brown" Wilken's interview after she escaped a house fire best encapsulates the latter. These maneuvers, especially when applied to Black women and girls, position their actions as exaggerated and excessive enough that others can embody them to express their own emotional lives.

The distortion of digital activism for Breonna Taylor also highlights the continued need to conflate Black women and girls with hypersexuality to "make a point." That meme creators thought it was lighthearted to plaster a call for police arrests on a Black woman's buttocks is clear evidence of misogynoir. In her article, Retta also notes,

> The fact still remains, however, that Taylor's name needed to be Photoshopped onto a singer's near-naked body in order to make an impression on some internet users (who may have otherwise ignored a petition or a plea for justice), while other names, such as Floyd's, didn't need to be subjected to such treatment.

Breonna Taylor's meme distortion illustrates how viral misogynoir travels in an environment where multiple relational scripts prevent Black women and girls from being seen as embodied beings with subjectivity. This is evidenced in the use of digital blackface, which is a part of the ongoing tendency to see Black women and girls as avatars. Also, this attempt at affective digital activism would not have needed to happen had the same elevated outrage that was given to George Floyd and Ahmaud Abrery been sustained for Breonna Taylor. Additionally, the distortion of the campaign into a satirical meme that uses hypersexualized imagery as titillation is evidence of the digital racist scopic regime Black women and girls must labor under. Finally, the white supremacy baked into the digital realm makes it impossible to hold and maintain respectful discourse when encountering Black women and girls' positionality.

OPPRESSION OLYMPICS

Following the McKinney pool party incident, I, two cisgender Black scholars, and one Black transgender man were asked to appear on the Marc Steiner Show, a local Baltimore public radio news program. The guest host, Professor Karsonya Whitehead, invited us all to discuss the footage and its meaning in Black cultural life. As we jointly discussed the intersection of racism and sexism impacting Black women and girls, each of us described the impact of seeing a barely clothed Black girl straddled by an adult white male with a gun. When we finished giving our assessments, the phone lines were opened for callers. An older Black male activist caller admonished me for bringing up the fact that Americans, including Black citizens, have difficulty recognizing Gender-Based Violence. He also took offense at one of the other panelists who provided facts about the lack of resources provided for girls who are incarcerated, compared to well-funded programs for boys. His critique,

> We do an injustice to ourselves when we talk about whose pain is worst; when we talk about prioritizing Black women over men, we have to make sure that we don't get into a play of who suffers more 'cause systems dehumanizes all black life.

At this statement, I replied,

> Bringing up the issues that impact women do not invisibilize the issues that impact men; we are not playing Oppression Olympics. The Combahee River Collective made the case, if you understand the intersection of anti-blackness and sexism, you have a road to liberation. We must turn to Black women to understand how the nexus of racism and sexism plays out; it's a matter of being able to look at the intersections of inequities in women's lives to recognize where we have a chance for liberation of all.

This public exchange is extremely important because it highlights one of the quintessential aspects fomenting viral misogynoir—the inability to mobilize outrage over Black women and girls' viral pain into action. In her 2016 TED talk, critical race scholar, Kimberlé Crenshaw facilitated an audience exercise that revealed how few of the activists, policymakers and thought makers in the room knew the names of Black women and girls killed by police. She notes,

> Communications experts tell us that when facts do not fit with the available frames, people have a difficult time incorporating new facts into their way of thinking about a problem. These women's names have slipped through our consciousness because there are no frames for us to see them, no frames for us to remember them, no frames for us to hold them. As a consequence, report- ers don't lead with them, policymakers don't think about them, and politicians aren't encouraged or demanded that they speak to them. (TED Talk 2016)

Crenshaw then introduces the concept of intersectionality: how both racism and sexism negatively impact Black women and girls' lives. She encour- ages activists to use intersectionality as a framework to help visibilize Black women's and girls' pain. In my analysis of viral misogynoir, I believe an intersectional framing and education about the deep legacy of Black women's activism against gender-based violence will move the needle forward. Black women's activism against sexual assault, incest, intimate partner violence and other forms of gender-based violence have been the fulcrum for the past and in the present Black civil rights movements. In discussing the 1944 case of Recy Taylor, a young Black woman who was raped by a group of white men as she came home from church, Danielle L. McGuire makes the links between the long history of Black women's activism against sexual violence and the wins of the civil rights era. She argues for testimony as a form of direct action to challenge the status quo. The willingness of Black women to testify about crimes against their complex personhood was essential to organizing campaigns during the civil rights era. To combat viral misogy- noir in the present, the framing must center the utility of advocacy against Gender-Based Violence.

SPECTACULARIZED LANGUAGE AND DOG WHISTLE POLITICS

The language we use to discuss gender-based violence also plays a part in embedding viral misogynoir. Our language reflects a culture that does not acknowledge gender-based violence. In the case of Donald Trump framing his videotaped declaration to "grab her by the p*ssy" as merely "locker room talk" erases the sexual assault inherent in his statement. In the fall of 2018, CNN's Carrie Severino, a lawyer for the Judicial Crisis Network, a group backing Supreme Court Justice nominee Brett Kavanaugh, said Christine Blasey Ford's rape allegations could describe "a whole range of conduct, from boorishness to rough horseplay to actual attempted rape." Dismissing violence as horseplay contributes to rape culture: a climate in which survivors are discouraged from coming forward and their experiences are discounted or disbelieved. Teasing out the differences between the NYT exposé on Harvey Weinstein by Jodi Kantor and Megan Twohey and the exposé by Ronan Farrow for *The New Yorker*, Constance Grady accurately suggests, "the vocabulary we have for gender-based violence tends to be either clinical but vague or graphic but specific" (Grady 2017).

Media culture rarely discusses sexual violence without trivializing it, obfuscating the systems that enable it, or turning it into spectacle. The less specific the language is, the more invisible the violence becomes. For example, the phrase, "he touched her genitals" sounds fairly innocuous, while the more specific language, "he grabbed her genitals" is more sensational. The latter could easily fit into a viral narrative of spectacularized violence. When Black women and girls experience gender-based violence, misogynoir further obscures its reality and its harmful impact on Black lives.

Dog whistle politics is the practice of "speaking in code to a target audience" (Lopez 2014) through seemingly neutral messages that warn about or denigrate certain social groups and classes (4). Dog whistle politics allows racism to persist despite a social climate in which citizens readily condemn any obvious form of racial acrimonies such as epithets or physical violence. This political rhetoric can be applied to any marginalized group who are perceived to be experiencing social progress (queer communities, immigrants, women, disabled people). It is often used strategically to further the majority group's political domination. Megan Kelly's glib comment that Dajerria Becton "was no saint" relies on sexism and racism to foster white political domination. To frame someone as a saint is to assume one is pure and innocent of all wrongdoing. Saints are hardworking, virtuous individuals. A saint may become a martyr but is never truly a victim because their sacrifice is ultimately a gift of reification to a higher power. An unruly Black female body is never pure enough to garner sainthood status, especially if it questions white domination by "talking back." Unruly Black females must also contend with being seen as hypersexual and deviant—traits unworthy of sainthood. By referring to Becton as not a saint Kelly also bolsters the rhetoric that says a woman or girl must be "pure" to truly be a victim. Kelly's language awards righteous political dominance to law enforcement, which uses both sexism and racism to obscure Gender-Based Violence against Black women and girls.

Ex-officer Daniel Holtzclaw was convicted of eighteen counts of rape, sexual battery, forcible oral sodomy, and other charges against eight different Black women. He admitted to running background checks on women with outstanding warrants or other criminal records to methodically target them for abuse. As Leigh Gilmore argues, "we should remember also that 'he said/ she said,' simply identifies how witnesses in an adversarial legal structure are positioned" (Gilmore 2017). The rhetoric of gender-based violence is such that "victim-blaming has the epistemological status of an objective and ethical response" (8). One of the ways we must broaden this discussion is by being able to better recognize and call out the tactics of those who have been accused. DARVO stands for "deny, attack, and reverse victim and offender"—a reaction that perpetrators may display in response to being held accountable for their behavior (Freyd 2013). This can occur when a guilty perpetrator assumes the role of "falsely accused" and attacks the accuser's credibility and blames the accuser of being the perpetrator of a false accusation. Even the legal rhetoric of gender-based violence enables misogynoir to exist in viral environments. Victims of gender-based violence are already called upon to prove their innocence, and when victim-blaming attaches itself to the complex history of Black women and girls' encounters with law enforcement, it becomes easy to deny sainthood to a 15-year-old girl in a bikini, and a 51-year-old woman on the side of the road.

A MULTIPLICITY OF STORIES

#MeToo is the culmination of decades of advocacy. The wave of #MeToo allegations in the past few years, and the varying rigor with which they have been reported, have prompted discourse about the lines between date rape and bad sex, between emotional abuse and tyranny. These conversations are difficult, but they ultimately strengthen the movement. While the conversations that are happening can leave us with more questions than answers, they are leading us to think *more* about our behaviors and previously accepted power dynamics, not less. Viral misogynoir gains currency when encounters centering Black women and girls become a part of a uniform narrative of spectacular violence. The viral video news cycle is quick to fit these stories into a repetitive cycle of indignation and inaction. By doing so, viral video consumption collapses Black women's and girls' narratives into the larger #BlackLivesMatter movement or fashions them into an overall critique of law enforcement's uses of force. While these incidents certainly are a part of these larger narratives, the outrage culture surrounding them obfuscates the complex matrices of power that impact Black women and girls. Additionally, we must fight to make Black pain legible is filtered through the narratives of mainstream society, which center masculine experiences. Philando Castile, Eric Garner, Alton Sterling, and Walter Scott all died on camera and their deaths at the hands of the police are legible. Sexual violence and gender-based violence are not as legible. We must not only recognize

Officer Eric Casebolt's actions as excessive force; we must also specifically identify Casebolt's acts of gender-based violence in dragging Becton's bikini-clad body across the grass and straddling her.

Black women and girls are not afforded the purity of victimhood that garners sentimental readings of their pain. Empty empathy occurs when we are invited to empathize with individuals who experience trauma without being provided the larger context for the existence of their trauma. In a society of spectacle, we tend to read stories of gender-based violence as singular episodes rather than as evidence of systemic oppression. But context matters now more than ever.

Chapter 2

Misogynoir and Media Culture

Using a combination of industry critique, textual analysis, and auto-ethnography, this chapter examines the 2015 F. Gary Gray film, *Straight Outta Compton* to argue our current measures of Black representational progress depend in perpetuating misogynoir within a sexist and racist cinematic landscape. I then provide potential corrective frameworks for gauging Black representational progress in Hollywood.

INTRODUCTION

Media culture filters stories of Black women and girls through racist and sexist lenses. When Black women's sexuality is fictionalized for entertainment, these same lenses often position their sexuality as monstrous and excessive, rendering them abject in comparison to Western notions of femininity. This move helps to solidify notions of racial difference between Blacks and all other races (Collins 27). When Black women and girls tell their truths about sexual violence within their own communities, the blame is often shifted onto them rather than the perpetrators due to the volatile mix of historical racism and sexism within Black communities.

As one who teaches media studies, I often begin my introduction to the idea of media culture with definitions provided by Douglass Kellner. A media culture is a world where images, sounds and spectacle shape aspects of our everyday lives (Kellner 1995) from our politics to our sense of identity. My students are often reluctant to accept the fact that much of the way they choose to live is influenced and sometimes even dependent upon the media with which they engage. To prove my point, I often have my students complete a weeklong media diary where they track the types and amounts of media they consume. By the end of that week, most of the students are shocked by how mediated images influence the way they dress, the slang they use, their expectations for their grades, and their social activities, including their group spiritual practices. Only after they have absorbed this knowledge do I begin conversations about the distortions inherent in the images and sounds they engage, and the systems of production that allow these images to saturate the market.

HOLLYWOOD INDUSTRY AND THE POPULAR

Cultural hegemonies occur when a ruling class dominates a diverse society's cultural output. Media (film, television, music, entertainment) is a key tool for maintaining cultural hegemonies. Those who control the media have the tools to concretize cultural power, making cultural texts sites of contestations amongst various groups and class blocs (Kellner 1971). Sites of hegemony are always in a state of flux because groups and class blocks change over time (Hall, 1986), however, hegemonic change comes slowly for some industries. As a part of a broader media industry, Western cinema is organized on a model of mass production designed to attract profit for large corporations. For a film to be deemed successful in the industry at minimum, the text must receive critical evaluations, have a strong financial performance, and/or receive symbolic accolades such as awards (Simonton 2009). When film and television is produced en masse for a corporation's profit, it is extremely important that these texts follow conventional codes, rules and formulas that support those who hold hegemonic power. These codes and rules extend not only to the content of the popular text but also to elements of its pre-production, production, and post-production cycle. Mediated images and sounds must elicit few surprises for the audience, be easily replicable, and uphold the values and ideologies of the time in which they are made. Western cinema hinges on uniform stories and modes of production that make the industry, audiences, and the dominate culture, feel stable and safe.

For most industries, Hollywood included, the days of standardization are waning. Standardization was "the model of leadership based on command and control, hierarchy and silos. The one that defined the measures of success for people, then rewarded only those who met those measures. It was about creating barriers, defining the narrative, putting people in boxes, and protecting the establishment" (Lolpis 2020). This was especially true in the "golden age" of Hollywood (1930s–1960s) when movie studios created specialized jobs to make filmmaking as economically efficient as possible. Standardization determined which actors worked for which studios, how scripts were created, as well as how films were rated, categorized, and promoted. Even after Hollywood moved to a blockbuster and franchise-driven model in the 1980s, standardization meant Hollywood had a keen understanding of how many films to make a year, which demographics would consume them, and how many sequels it would be able to make from one text. In the 1990s, studios like Miramax helped invigorate the Hollywood landscape by supporting independent films and new talent, but with the 2008 recession came a consolidation of previously separate niche studios. Since then, Hollywood has turned a profit by investing in widely advertised, spectacularized films that are well suited to multiplexes. Hollywood operates under a risk averse model which favors "presold concepts as budgets continue to skyrocket, ballooned. . . by the cost of promotion" (Koehler 2018), however, the overall standardization of the film industry is beginning to change.

Building off Stuart Hall's work on culture and hegemony, Molina Guzman describes Hollywood as, "a cultural institution informed by and informative of US social values and norms (2016, 439)." Hall argued the historical reproduction of "othering" through stereotypic binary representations of ethnic and racial difference is symptomatic of the hegemonic push and pull of power. Hollywood texts reflect implicit and explicit race and gender biases by those with the means to control its output. Guzman suggests, as a cultural institution, recent "contestations over the lack of diversity in Hollywood are indicative of broader social conflicts over the changing status of ethnicity, race, and gender" (440). The U.S. is currently undergoing a demographic shift. The majority of 6- to 21-year-olds are non-Hispanic whites and the U.S. Census has projected "a majority of the U.S. population will be nonwhite by the year 2050" (PEW 2019). The shift in demographics coincides with shifts in the way people produce and consume film and television. The global coronavirus pandemic of 2020 is only hastening changes in standardization. Prior to the coronavirus, global film audiences were shrinking despite theater owners' attempts to revamp the moviegoing experience with in-theater dining, more comfortable seating and other amenities meant to imitate the in-home viewing experience. According to the World Economic Forum, theater operators are also "challenged by a shrinking theatrical window, the amount of time studios show movies exclusively in theatres before releasing them for sale, download or streaming" (Hall and Pasquini 2020). Reflecting consumers' preferences for streaming video on demand, movie studios have begun creating products for the video on demand market and prioritizing the release of their own titles, which further pushes theaters out of the loop. Streaming services such as Netflix, Hulu, and Amazon Prime also create a need for cultural products that the shifting demographics will consume. This complicates the ongoing racial and ethnic hegemony of the Hollywood industry. Guzman surmises, "contemporary Hollywood is caught between the force of historically established white patriarchal structures of cultural production, and the rising currents of changing demographics, economics, and technology" (441). Internet and streaming services "are picking up Hollywood's slack" (Koehler 2018) around diverse options and niche film. Still, the white men who always ran the film industry continue to do so, hoarding high-status creative and commercial work as well as the lion's share of profits (Quinn 2020). These shifts in demographics and consuming habits may be considered progress for an industry that has long been dominated by the ruling class. However, if those who are "othered" by the ruling class are still positioned as outside the norm in film and television narratives and industry, how can these changes herald progress?

THE STATE OF BLACK HOLLYWOOD

We are in a watershed moment where Black cultural workers are increasingly able to tell Black narratives with funding from major studios and through independent funding from streaming services and video on demand studios eager for a diversity of content. The highly successful films *Black Panther* (Ryan Coogler 2018), and *A Wrinkle in Time* (Ava DuVernay, 2018) are just two examples. Black cultural workers (writers, singers, photographers, designers, and actors) are seeing their work not only distributed in theaters but also online, on streaming platforms, on cable and increasingly on prime-time television. Still, Hollywood is a contradictory and difficult space for Black cultural producers to navigate. Regardless of the demographic and consumer shifts occurring in the U.S., Black cultural products must still adhere to Hollywood's white patriarchal structures to be deemed successful. Hollywood's white patriarchal structure is fueled by the racialized logic that stories about Black people made by Black people are inherently un-bankable. This positionality creates a cycle where Hollywood does not invest in movies made about Black people by Black people which then proves their thesis that Black movies are not commercially successful. Often Black cultural workers who are deemed successful in Hollywood are positioned and position themselves, as somehow exceptional. An exploration of media articles about Hollywood's racial progress found 32 of 53 acknowledged improvements in Hollywood through "narratives of exceptional individuals who are able to brand themselves such as Shonda Rhimes, Lee Daniels and Paul Lee" (Guzman 444). Exceptional Black Hollywood cultural workers are those who not only market themselves as special, they also willingly allow themselves to be held up as such. This creates a scenario where improvements in TV representations of multicultural difference are associated with market demands, specifically the increasing diversification of US media audiences. Second, it equates the minimal on-screen visibility of marginalized groups with social progress thus creating the illusion that Hollywood's diversity is improving.

The Black Hollywood elite see themselves as such, which, even when deserved, creates a dangerous black exceptionalism paradox. When one group of Black cultural workers are held up as the exception, not the rule, the dominant class is able to believe in a myth of Hollywood racial progress—i.e., diversity. As Michele Alexander posits exceptional Black people provide evidence that race is no longer relevant (2010). Successful Black cultural workers know this is the case and brand themselves as exceptional while also finding ways to work around Hollywood's exclusion. Studying the career trajectories of two Hollywood icons, Will Smith and Tyler Perry, Ethine Quinn found, "fueling Overbrook's and Perry's focus on self-branding was a keen racial understanding of the film industry's under-resourcing of black productions" (203). The common argument is that the Black Hollywood elite such as Perry and Smith have helped increase "black employment in film [because] Black top talent, just like nonblack talent, develops informal networks [that] tend to be much more diverse than their white counterparts" (204). This sentiment is echoed through many articles about Hollywood's racial progress. Yet, discussing diversity in Hollywood, entertainment lawyer Jaia Thomas observed, "I have learned that many artists, even those who are the most vociferous advocates for diversity, often treat the makeup of their own teams as an afterthought" (2020). Diversity in Hollywood in inconsistent and wholly dependent on market forces and symbolic wins. A brief look at trends in Black film by decade illustrates this.

In the 1970s, Blaxploitation cinema emerged in reaction to the abandonment of metropolitan areas by whites following the civil rights uprisings in the 1960s and government divestment in urban areas. Movie theater audiences in cities became primarily Black and Brown. This opportunity allowed independent B-movies written, produced, and starring Black people to be shown, signaled by Melvin Van Peeple's *Sweetsweet Back's Bad Ass Song*. Once Hollywood industry saw that there was an audience willing to pay for Black film, it invested in the genre—wresting creative control from the mainly Black cultural producers while still attracting Black audiences. In the 1980s, Eddie Murphy and Bill Cosby's crossover commercial success dovetailed with the mainstreaming of hip-hop, indicating that there were non-Black consumers of Black culture. This helped pave the way in the 1990s for Hollywood to declare racism won, evidenced by the New Black film renaissance. The New Black film renaissance ushered in by John Singleton's 1991 film, *Boyz in the Hood*, led to 17 Black led films released by mainstream studios—a first for Hollywood. Once white-helmed Hollywood remembered "it could make big profits on black films, there was a frenzy for material, leading to such films as *Juice, Malcolm X*, and *Passenger 57*" (Barboza 2016). By the mid-to-late 1990s, the number of Black helmed films had sharply declined until 2002, when Hollywood once again declared racism won. That year, Academy Awards were given to Halle Berry, Denzel Washington, and the legendary Sidney Poitier. Cultural studies scholar David

Leonard recalls, "Hollywood insiders and critics alike cited this supposedly historic moment as a sign of America's racial progress" (2006). Since 2016, Hollywood has been investing in Black cultural workers. Yet, a recent article in *Hollywood Reporter* comparing the watershed diversity of 2018 with Black helmed films in 2019, show that Hollywood's commitment to diversity did not directly carry over to the next year. In fact, "the share of Black directors dropped more than five points from 2018, when they made up 10.7 percent of the filmmakers behind the top Hollywood films. People of color were under-represented at every stage in the making of 2019's highest-grossing films" (Jarvey 2020, 53). The cyclical nature of Black success in Hollywood illustrates depictions of ethnic and racial minorities may be improving but those who make executive decisions are still overwhelmingly represented by the dominant class, and its obsession with market forces. A focus on increasing representational diversity assumes that demographic change will result in the structural transformation of the industry. This is not necessarily true.

THE HOLLYWOOD JIM CROW

There are more images of Black people made by Black people available to the masses, yet, as Maryann Erigha points out, "symbolic and numerical representation. . . can be present [and still not alleviate] inequalities" (Erigha 2019). Structural inequalities such as the isolation of Black directors from white Hollywood prevent Black cultural producers from *maintaining* power in the industry. Erigha goes on to suggest racial progress in Hollywood must also take into consideration the ways filmic texts produce and recognize Black lives as a part of "dominant cultural myths, narratives and images" in U.S. citizenship. These turns would directly challenge Western cinema's ongoing "othering" of non-whites by awarding of cultural citizenship to Black consumers. Unfortunately, in our current Hollywood landscape, a disproportionate number of Black cultural narratives focus their energy on reifying the citizenship of Black men, leaving stories of Black women and girls on the margins.

Despite Hollywood's recent willingness to provide funding to Black female artists such as Ava DuVernay, Issa Rae, and Janet Mock, most Black male directors write stories about, and for, Black men. In recent years, organizations such as the Geena Davis Institute on Gender in Media and the New York Film Academy (NYFA) have been researching and releasing information about the impact of gender inequality in mainstream American entertainment. NYFA found that there is a 5.4 percent increase in female characters on-screen when the director is a woman, and the average ratio of male actors to female actors is 2.3:1. Additionally, scripts had 7x more male writers than female writers in 2017. In the documentary, *This Changes Everything,* Geena Davis posits, "80% of the media consumed worldwide is created in the United States. We are responsible for exporting a pretty negative view of women around the world" (2019). Black female directors represent "less than 1% of directors of contemporary Hollywood movies, and no Black woman has sustained a successful career primarily through directing Hollywood movies" (Erigha ch.3). Female directors are often saddled with smaller budgets and limited international exposure. For Black female directors this is even more pronounced. The lack of stories about the interior lives of Black women told by Black women makes Black female directors some of the most marginalized professionals in the industry. Unpacking the role of Black directors in Hollywood, Melvin Donalson suggests there is a concern that "if black directors fail to develop black-oriented material, those projects will not be made [because] white directors don't display a passion to tell stories about African American experiences" (279). For Black directors to have success in Hollywood they must also be able to make content that white audiences also want to see, making "crossover appeal" the measure with Hollywood success is judged. This means the work of Black filmmakers is also to create work that is highly accessible to non-Black audiences while also affirming a connection to Black audiences.

For all intents and purpose, the 2015 F. Gary Gray film, *Straight Outta Compton,* meets the definition of Hollywood racial progress. 1) It was directed by a Black man; 2) it told a story about a moment in Black cultural history that was vital to the story of the U.S. as a whole; 3) it employed a racially diverse production team; 4) the film had crossover audience appeal, making millions of dollars and 5) it received multiple symbolic representational victories. In *Straight Outta Compton*, F. Gary Gray tells the complicated and politically charged story of rap group N. W. A. (Niggas With Attitudes) in the mid-1980s. Upon the film's release, Ava DuVernay, Hollywood's most powerful Black female director, tweeted, "to be a woman who loves hip hop at times is to be in love with your abuser. Because the music was and is that. And yet the culture is ours." She goes on to praise F. Gary Gray's depiction of that particular time, noting, "all the stifling of our voices as young black people in that place at that time while a war was going on against us. @FGaryGray captured it " (2015). In those two tweets, DuVernay captured the exact feelings I had while viewing this film. *Straight Outta Compton* garnered praise from its release and through the awards season, where it was nominated for an Academy Award for Best Original Screenplay and was awarded Movie of the Year from the American Film Institute. It is a story deserving of acclaim. It captured a moment in time where the war on young Black people was violent and unforgiving, and it made logical visual leaps to our current climate where young Black people continue to be disenfranchised. The film celebrated the beautiful, and sometimes playful, cultural resistance that only hip-hop and funk music seem to capture authentically. It provided scenes of the circumstances that Black people must wrestle with as we punch self-definition out of the concrete foundation that is America's war on Blackness. With its success, *Straight Outta Compton* appears to be an example of Hollywood racial progress. But how can a text rife with misogynoir be progress? And if it is, who is progressing on the backs of whom?

STRAIGHT OUTTA MISOGYNOIR: A TEXTUAL ANALYSIS

The misogynoir within *Straight Outta Compton* began in pre-production, evident from the leaked racist and sexist casting call created by Sande Allesi Casting (Cadet 2014).

SAG OR NON-UNION FEMALES - PLEASE SEE BELOW FOR SPECIFIC BREAKDOWN. DO NOT EMAIL IN FOR MORE THAN ONE CATEGORY:
A GIRLS: These are the hottest of the hottest. Models. MUST have real hair - no extensions, very classy looking, great bodies. You can be Black, White, Asian, Hispanic, Mid-eastern, or Mixed race too. Age 18–30. Please email a current color photo, your name, Union status, height/weight, age, city in which you live and phone number to: SandeAlessiCasting@gmail.com subject line should read: A GIRLS
B GIRLS: These are fine girls, long natural hair, really nice bodies. Small waists, nice hips. You should be light-skinned. Beyonce is a prototype here. Age 18–30. Please email a current color photo, your name, Union status, height/weight, age, city in which you live and phone number to: SandeAlessiCasting@gmail.com subject line should read: B GIRLS
C GIRLS: These are African American girls, medium to light-skinned with a weave. Age 18–30. Please email a current color photo, your name, Union status, height/weight, age, city in which you live and phone number to: SandeAlessiCasting@gmail.com subject line should read: C GIRLS
D GIRLS: These are African American girls. Poor, not in good shape. Medium to dark skin tone. Character types. Age 18–30. Please email a current color photo, your name, Union status, height/weight, age, city in which you live and phone number to: SandeAlessiCasting@gmail.com subject line should read: D GIRLS

In her review of the film for *Ms. Magazine*, Janell Hobson refers to this casting call as a "racial and color hierarchy of women's bodies" (Hobson 2015) and she could not be more accurate. The "best of the best" are positioned as belonging to a spectrum of racial identities, while "D" girls, those at the very bottom of the hierarchy, are coded specifically medium to dark-skinned African-Americans. Colorism is a key component of controlling images. A 2012 longitudinal study of colorism and family dynamics found lighter-skinned daughters received higher-quality parenting compared to those with darker skin (Lander, Simons, et al., 2013). The political, psychological, and economic domination of Black women hinges on these aspects of colorism.

The misogynoir in *Straight Outta Compton* also stems from the dearth of fleshed out, well-rounded, female characters. Only four female actors have speaking roles. Lisa Rennee Pitts, who played Dr. Dre's long-suffering mother (Verna Griffin), and Carra Patterson, who portrayed Eazy-E's wife (Tomica Woods-Wright) are the only women afforded more than three minutes of screen time. When Lavetta, the mother of Dr. Dre's first child confronts him about his neglect, she is portrayed as hysterical and out of line. Dr. Dre's response to her valid critique is to admonish her for her bad timing. The scene is then quickly followed up by an encounter between the group and law enforcement, directing victimhood status to the male characters, not the female characters. Women are collateral damage in N. W. A's. rise to fame.

Misogynoir is also evident in the lack of critique of misogyny in N. W. A's music. Unnamed, silent women are featured in the studios, hotel rooms, and pool parties where the actors spout lyrics such as, *"Went to her house to get her out of the pad. Dumb hoe says something stupid that made me mad"* (Ice Cube 1987). These lyrics suggest the women in their lives are all imbeciles, and this misogyny is made worse by the fact that these background women are never properly identified as family members, entertainers, or groupies. In this same song, the rappers add, *"She started talkin' shit, wouldn't you know? Reached back like a pimp and slapped the hoe."* None of the female characters in the film react to hearing these lyrics, in fact, a point is made to show them actively singing the songs. Discussing Spike Lee's film, *School Daze* and the popularity of the song, Da Butt by E. U., bell hooks refer to the song as playful, cultural, nationalist resistance. She then says, "its potential to disrupt and challenge notions of black bodies, specifically female bodies, was undercut by the overall sexual humiliation and abuse of black females in the film" (hooks 2015, 1992). The same analysis applies to *Straight Outta Compton.* The director and screenwriters missed the opportunity to make visible Black female fans of hip-hop by portraying women as voiceless, submissive groupies, and not as real hip-hop fans who wrestle with enjoying and critiquing the work.

Finally, misogynoir is compounded by F. Gary Gray's responses to those who critiqued the horrible treatment of the few women in the film, and the exclusion of Dr. Dre's history as a woman-batterer. Dre's infamous 1991 assault on *Pump It Up* journalist, Dee Barnes, was stricken from the final cut of the film. At a press event, when asked why this story and other incidents of misogyny were excluded or downplayed, F. Gary Gray suggested they had to narrow the story down for length and focus on the "main" narrative, which was about all the members of N. W. A, not just Dr. Dre. He said, "it wasn't about a lot of side stories," (Lockett 2015). The concept of N. W. A.'s negative treatment of Black women was not exclusive to just Dr. Dre. If misogynoir was not essential to the revenue and popularity of the group, why create songs such as "A Bitch Is a Bitch" or "She Swallowed It"? Additionally, fear of excess length/side story did not prevent the director from including fictitious scenes where Black groupies in orgies were manhandled and disrespected. One of the most notable fictional instances occurred when a dark-skinned actress, given the name Felicia, is interrupted while performing fellatio on Eazy-E. She is summarily kicked out of the hotel room, naked after her boy-friend confronts the group with a gun. For added measure, Ice Cube cuffs her across the head, saying "Bye, Felicia," a notable line from Ice Cube's classic film, *Friday* (1996). Misogynoir is essential to lending *Straight Outta Compton* "authenticity," but only if the consequences of the misogynoir are downplayed as harmless, or if Black female hip-hop enthusiasts are framed as a voiceless monolith. This is how misogynoir works in media culture. It is evidence of our cultural capacity to use Black women's bodies as a site for the enactment of patriarchal masculinity on film when that masculinity is secured through violence, colorism, and silencing. Misogynistic narratives are often the default in stories about Black hip-hop and urban culture. From Dr. Dre's long-suffering matriarchal figure, Verna Griffin, to Easy E's light-skinned, racially ambiguous wife, Tomica Woods-Wright, to Dr. Dre's sapphire baby mama, Cassandra Joy Green, all the way to pool parties filled with dark-skinned jezebel groupies—misogynoir helps these stories travel, further encoding a default narrative in our psyche. Without explicit scenes of characters negotiating mediated images of Black female pain, films such as *Straight Outta Compton* re-inscribe that pain onto Black women viewers. White dominated Hollywood has racialized logics that concretize structural inequality. While there are many frameworks with which to analyze mediated images within media culture, the frameworks designed to specifically understand the lives of Black women and girls must work *overtime* to trace the threads of distorted socio-historical movements that have shaped them. The success of misogynoir laden *Straight Outta Compton* in the eyes of Black and white Hollywood alike suggests that it is time to complicate markers of racial progress. It is time for markers that are not contingent solely on increased Black presence in front of and behind the camera, studio profits, or attaining symbolic representational wins (awards) within a racist and sexist Hollywood landscape.

COMPLICATING BLACK REPRESENTATIONAL PROGRESS

Media represents our social reality, providing and reflecting our ever-changing understanding of our social and group identities. For years, scholars, makers and consumers of Black cultural text have debated the role of popular film and television in advancing Black representational progress. The notion of progress presumes, "society is ameliorative—gradually moving toward perfection—through incremental reforms or social action" (Seamster and Ray 2018, 1365). The markers with which "progress" is determined change over time and according to the standpoint of those studying the notion. In studies of race in the U.S., racial progress is often determined by measuring how close Black people are to mirroring the health, economic, educational, and cultural attainment of the dominate class—white people. Most discussion of Black representation in media build upon this framework which sees progress as always linear and moving toward improvement. From Donald Bogle (1973, 2016) and Ed Guerrero's (1993) historical surveys of Black American representation in film and television, to bell hooks' critical theories on spectatorship within a white supremacist hetero-patriarchy (1992, 2015), one of the essential debates has been about the role of Black cultural workers in accurately portraying Black people on screen at any given time. If D. W. Griffith's 1915 film, *Birth of a Nation* "constituted the playbook for Hollywood's representation of Black manhood, womanhood, its obsession with miscegenation and its fixing of [Black] people within certain spaces" (Diawara 1993), then Black representational progress is the perpetual effort of Black cultural workers to create counterimages to these concrete visual ideals.

Burden of Representation

According to Shohat and Stam, the burden of representation occurs whenever a marginalized or underrepresented group is portrayed in film. This burden is "at once religious, esthetic, political and semiotic" (182) and it has a lasting impact on the viewer, especially if the viewer is a member of the marginalized group. Discussing the work of early Black filmmakers like Oscar Micheaux, Pearl Bowser and Louise Spence suggests Black cultural workers have long labored under a burden of representation. Born out of a desire for assimilation and acceptance, Black cultural workers have been tasked with telling stories that paint a positive image of Black life to combat negative images created by an industry dominated by the white gaze. In the early days of cinema, Black filmmakers found themselves inhibited in their storytelling so much so that they were unable to show the diversity of Black experiences. Filmmakers were deemed disloyal to the race when they focused on telling stories of the "downtrodden, the oppressed, and social embarrassments" (2000, 6). Social embarrassment could include anything from stories of sexual violence or gambling to stories about experiencing the struggles of urban and rural poverty. The burden of representation illuminates the bind of Black cultural workers who were tasked with creating compelling stories that did not concretize notions of Black pathology or suggests, conversely, that the only stories worth producing were those that highlighted upwardly mobile Black people. The early films of Oscar Micheaux, "deflated the pretensions of the expanding black middle class by providing images of victimization and poverty too reminiscent of racist portrayals that were supposedly defining characteristics of the race and the essence of the African American condition" (6). Black filmmakers were expected to combat negative representation by showing the world the existence of a Black middle class. This, among many others was the reason Black film critics and viewers disparaged much of Micheaux's pioneering works. However, these controversies also helped facilitate Micheaux's unique approaches to storytelling. For example, in his 1921 film, *Body and Soul*, he was able to show the corruption of the Black church by making most of the story take place within a dream.

It is important to note that the classic Hollywood industry was run largely by immigrant populations who also used moving images to solidify their status as assimilated and upwardly mobile. Thus, many classic Hollywood movies were awash in a fantasy of assimilation. The tensions experienced by Black cultural workers in the early days of cinema conflicted with the notion that an authentic Black identity was working-class and mainly associated with folk culture. Black people, as the most abject on the white screen, longed for stories that presented them with more opportunity than their everyday experiences as much as immigrant whites. Successful Black filmmakers continue to navigate debates about the medium's role in elevating Black social class or countering myths of Black pathology.

Black arts poet Larry Neal believed that the key to addressing this bind was the creation of a Black aesthetic, a set of criteria created by Black people for Black cultural texts that would take into consideration a film's ability to be socially uplifting while also reflecting the social realities of Black life. A Black aesthetic notes the monetary constraints of Black film production, and the relationship between the text and the Black audience, which may or may not run counter to those who produced it. Firmly embedded in the concept of a Black film aesthetic is the need for Black people to have full control over the means of production. Yet, one need only look at the short life history of

Blaxploitation films to recognize that having Black people in front of and behind the camera does, "not necessarily track with an 'increased' Black cinematic perspective" (Lawrence and Butters, Jr. 2016). Controlling the means of production does not ensure representational progress, so arguments that make representation the goal need to be complicated.

The Promise of Representation

Often discourse about Black representational progress is linked more to the increased visibility of a diverse cohort of Black people on the screen. Discussing the popularity of "magical negro" narratives in Western cinema, Matthew Hughey notes visibility and acceptance is, "not a guarantee of legitimacy or decency, but it is a precondition of regimes of surveillance. The dominant features of previous social orders—restrictive Jim Crow folkways and *de jure* racism—were clearly articulated through media images. Today, media exercises no less an influence in promulgating and protecting *de facto* racism through the patterned combination of white normativity and antiblack stereotypes under the guise of progressive black-white friendships that supposedly indicate improving race relations" (544). Even when more varied Black characters are visible, they are still bound by the biases and interests of whomever controls the narrative. Black cultural workers are tasked with providing Black audiences roadmaps to liberation from anti-black oppression by showcasing the myriad of ways Black people are progressing. Discussing Spike Lee's films as cultural engineering, William Harris claims the director is concerned with "aspects of our interpersonal and collective behavior" and as such, uses his films "for the purpose of deflecting human habit in the new direction of new and perhaps constructive endeavors" (24). There is promise in the notion that by seeing a wide range of Black people tackling oppression from multiple standpoints, Black people will better be able to navigate white-racist heteropatriarchy. Unfortunately, much of the conversation about representation is subsumed by binary notions that pit representation against diversity and inclusion.

Representation vs. Diversity

On a 2018 episode of *The Daily Show with Trevor Noah*, Emmy award-winning actor, Riz Ahmed broke down his understanding of the difference between representation and diversity. The Pakistani-British actor said, "I don't like to talk about diversity. I feel like it sounds like an added extra. It sounds like the fries, not the burger. It sounds like something on the side. You got your main thing going on, and you sprinkle a little bit of diversity on top of that. That's not what it's about for me. It's about representation. And representation is fundamental in terms of what we expect from our culture and from our politics. We all want to feel represented. We all want to feel seen and heard and valued. So, I prefer to talk about representation" (2018). To Ahmed, representation is about being validated as a fully complex and actualized human while diversity is checking off a box for the appearance of inclusion. In essence, advocating for diversity is about equality for equality's sake. While his sentiment is sound, the dichotomous nature of his analysis is not. Representation and diversity should not be separated in such a binary way. It suggests the distinction between mirror narratives and window narratives in children's books. Books that are considered mirrors reflect people's lives back to them and help them form group identity. Windows are books that provide insight into those whose experiences differ from one's own. Without a *diversity* of people in front of and behind the camera, both mirror and window narratives suffer. In September 2020 Commissioner Allison Herris Lee conducted a talk about diversity at Security and Exchange Commission. She noted, "companies with the greatest ethnic diversity on executive teams outperformed those with the least by 36 percent in profitability. The same report found that companies with more than 30 percent women on their executive teams are significantly more likely to outperform those with fewer or no women executives. Companies with higher-than-average diversity on management teams report higher revenue from new products and services. More women in senior positions is associated with higher return on assets" (10). Hollywood is an industry run by corporations so the same economic logics about corporations are applicable to discussions of representation in Hollywood. Diversity is good for Hollywood's bottom line and reputation as an industry.

Critiques of Hollywood's lack of diversity rose to a fever pitch in the summer of 2020 following multiple uprising in the wake of the death of George Floyd. Countless corporations released statements calling for diversity and inclusion, including many corporations directly engaged in the entertainment industry. Many of these statements called attention to the structural inequities that fuel Hollywood's lack of representation. For example, Black filmmakers and executives interviewed by the *Los Angeles Times* all lamented, "the stark absence of black executives in studios' ranks" (Faughnder and Perman 2020). Articles in *Variety, Hollywood Reporter,* and the *Los Angeles Times* supported their features on diversity with data from the *Anneberg Inclusion Initiative* which has been collecting Hollywood's diversity and inclusion data for several years to make structural arguments about diversity. Since the #OscarsSoWhite awareness campaign began in 2016, discussions about diversity have expanded beyond calls for more representation of diverse populations onscreen, to a call for the inclusion of more diverse populations in structural positions in Hollywood. In September 2020, the Academy of Arts and Motion Pictures released new criteria for Best Picture to address the lack of diversity evident in the Best Picture categories. According to the Academy, "The aperture must widen to reflect our diverse global population in both the creation of motion pictures and in the audiences, who connect with them. The Academy is committed to playing a vital role in helping make this a reality," said Academy President David Rubin and Academy CEO Dawn Hudson in a statement. "We believe these inclusion standards will be a catalyst for long-lasting, essential change in our industry" (Oscars 2020).

The rules go into full effect in 2024 and demands films meet at least two of four new standards that stipulate roles both onscreen and behind the scenes be filled by people from underrepresented groups, including race, women, LGBTQ, and people with cognitive or physical disabilities, including the deaf and hard of hearing (Oscars 2020). When the rules were released, several Hollywood personalities spoke out for and against them.

"I fully support @TheAcademy's new representation and inclusion standards for Oscars eligibility," tweeted prolific film producer and Latin America Oscars preshow host Axel Kuschevatzky, adding that the new rules were "important."

"The Academy is finally—finally!—doing something to ensure that under-represented groups have a shot," wrote culture critic Sonny Bunch on Twitter, pointing out that the past four years of Best Picture wins featured cast and crew from those groups.

Those opposed to the new rules were outspoken as well. Actress Kirstie Alley responded,

"The new RULES to qualify for 'best picture' are dictatorial... anti-artist... Hollywood you're swinging so far left you're bumping into your own a**"

And actor Dean Cain wrote, "How about we judge on this criteria—which film was the BEST PICTURE?" and "when do we start handing out participation Oscars?" (*Forbes* 2020). Cain's response eerily mimics arguments against affirmative action policies designed to increase opportunities for those who have experienced structural inequities in the past. It is as if addressing structural inequities immediately disenfranchises the dominant caste. By invoking the idea of "participation Oscars" he assumes the new criteria for Best Picture de-legitimizes the exclusivity of the coveted Best Picture award.

Spike Lee's response to negative feedback was to say, "the Oscar voters who flat out oppose the new set of rules "probably voted for 'Driving Miss Daisy' and 'Green Book'" (*Variety* 2020). Lee's dismissal of these critiques calls attention to the type of diversity Riz Ahmed is lamenting—equality that maintains the status quo where white dominated, sentimental storytelling is hailed as diverse storytelling. Another, somewhat wary support for the Oscar's new categories came from Kellie Nicole Terrell, the head of communications for the #MeToo Movement. She tweeted, "like affirmative action, this new (however well-intentioned?) Academy rule will mostly benefit white female directors who will act brand new about this advantage," and "in order to win an Oscar, you still have to have the resources and access to make a feature film" (Twitter 2020). Terrell's critique is a much more intersectional approach to understanding how even structural approaches to increasing representation and diversity still have the potential to leave those who inhabit various social identities at a disadvantage. For example, in a 2006 article for the University of *Michigan Law Review*, law professor Kimberlé Crenshaw found, "the primary beneficiaries of affirmative action have been Euro-American women" (129). Structural fixes are not infallible because power-relations are ever-changing.

The term "politically correct" was originally used in leftist circles to ironically call attention to colleagues who were being dogmatic in their analysis. This inside joke designed to help progressives stay open to multiple interpretations was upended in the 1990s by conservatives who used it to claim there is a leftwing political agenda that has taken control of American universities and cultural institutions in a bid to end free speech. Behind conservative accusations of political correctness is an assumption that there exists a nefarious group of liberal elites determined to control your mind by controlling your words. Kristie Alley's assessment that the Oscar rules are akin to a dictatorship and Dean Cain's lumping them in with affirmative action and participation trophies really encapsulates resistance to the idea of structurally embedding diversity. Sometimes, opposition to increased representation or diversity and inclusion is a knee-jerk reaction to what is *perceived* as representational correctness.

Representational Correctness

Edward Shiappa (2008) defines representational correctness as "a set of beliefs that often implicitly underlies critiques of popular text that are less useful than they may appear to be" (2). In his book of the same name, he argues representational norms of accuracy (representation must be authentic and true to the social group depicted to avoid the distortion of stereotype), purity (representation must be pure in its liberatory possibilities and avoid ambivalence or ideological contradiction) and innocence (representation must be devoid of offense or insult to the group depicted) fuels a desire for screen representations of marginalized people that are "correct" in the eyes of the audience members who best identify with those social groups. Representational correctness thrives in a landscape where negative critiques carry more weight than positive critiques. Shiappa argues when a film text is called out as inaccurate or harmful in its representation of an underrepresented group, that film is somehow dismissed or canceled outright, which is inherently detrimental to discourse about representation and equality. While this sentiment bears some truth for texts that are not shielded by major Hollywood studios, the films that Spike Lee critiques in his response to the new Oscar rules—namely *Driving Miss Daisey* and *The Green Book* were far from canceled despite their representational flaws and sentimental narrative approaches to interracial friendships.

Shiappa also suggests a lack of commitment to audience research and too firm commitment to textual analysis in media studies bolsters calls for representational correctness. These two factors make for simplistic assumptions about the negative and positive effects of screen texts on audiences. While this may certainly be the case for some film projects, sociologists who look at the impact of media representation on issues ranging from social identity development to public health outcomes may beg to differ. The core of Shiappa's concern is that representational correctness will, "lead to an interpretive flexibility that makes it less likely that critics will ever perceive any progress in representations of minorities" (162). I agree that the quest for representational purity is an impossible and flawed standard to meet. To dismiss a text outright as representationally incorrect is to create a double bind that categorizes performances either as inaccurate/inauthentic or stereotypical.

There are several aspects of Shiappa's model that are of use in crafting a new approach to assessing Black representational progress. First and foremost is the awareness that it is faulty logic to presume there is a dominant way a media text is to be read. Secondly, that it is unhelpful to believe "correct" representation is that which meets the approval of the marginalized viewer who is reading it. Cultural and media scholars study film because everything in film is created by people. That means positionality, standpoints, norms, skills, and ideologies are the stuff that brings a text to life. This provides scholars the opportunity to show how a text is reflective of the time and standpoints in which it is made. Finally, his suggestion that texts are not judged by the tenants of accuracy, purity and innocence is a useful counter to those laboring under burden of representation. So, how does one critique an example of Hollywood representational progress like *Straight Outta Compton* without falling into the trap of demanding representational correctness? The first step is troubling the concept of authenticity.

THE BIND OF AUTHENTICITY

There is much debate about what represents an authentic portrayal of Black life on screen and off screen. Black people are not monolithic, Black popular culture cannot be separated into binaries of high art versus low art or authentic representation versus inauthentic representation (Hall 1981). Blackness is always determined by what is expected and needed from Black bodies at a

given time. At one point in our country's history, Blackness was determined
by the need to have a secure labor force for imperialist expansion. At other
points in time, media images of Black people as servants helped white communities cling to a feeling of superiority during the Great Depression that was
stripping them of their economic power. The efforts to pin down authentic
Blackness in cultural texts results in an overuse of performative signifiers of
Black identity, such as clothing, hair choices and linguistics. This is reflected
in the popularity of minstrelsy and Blackface at the turn of the twentieth century. As Dicker posits now, "with the commodification of African American
culture, Blackness has become an accessory that can be put on like burnt cork
and hog fat: baggy pants, overpriced athletic shoes, cornrows or dread locks,
gaudy jewelry, swiveling necks, snapping fingers, absent consonants "No you
dinent!" (Dicker 616). Recent controversies about non-Black people adopt-
ing Black identities, such as the case of Jessica Krug at George Washington
University, illuminate this ongoing phenomenon. A Jewish woman from
Kansas City, Krug adopted an Afro-Cuban persona to gain legitimacy as a
scholar in African American history. To secure academic and activist legitimacy, she willingly played into performative tropes of Blackness until she
was forced to reveal her identity. Not only does Krug represent performative
Blackness, but her story also shows how Black authenticity is intimately
linked to securing cultural capital. Although Black people are not monolithic,
it is still the case that to have Black cultural capital is to seem to have a connection with working-class Black communities. Discussing the creation of
the Buppie identity in the films of Spike Lee, Ruth Doughty notes,

> African American culture has traditionally been marked as a working-class phe-
> nomenon. From the slave stories, negro spirituals and customs of the Southern
> plantations to modern-day urban graffiti, street dance and rap performances,
> black culture is typically a product of the folk. Conversely, white American
> culture is a product of white, middle-class canonical elites. (125)

The problem with this dichotomy of working class versus middle class is
that it "stems from a belief that black economic mobility necessarily breeds
assimilationists and race traitors because of interracial mixing" (22). These
faulty links between racial and class identity concretizes flawed notions of
authentic Blackness, and feeds into the ethnographic impulse that sees stories
of Black life as an opportunity to safely watch the exotic and still primitive
"other" in action.

   When representing important moments of cultural history in film, the
burden of historical representation "requires that members of. . . underrepresented groups be portrayed in a way that allows the viewer to understand their
points of view, history, and language (Stoddard, Marcus 2006). Historical

films about marginalized populations and significant moments in history must make visible the complex lives and circumstances of those who are featured. The filmmaker's task is to bring life into a history that is often framed by the dominant caste. Movies like the 1998 film, *Mississippi Burning* which made white male FBI agents the heroes the Black civil rights movement are indicative of dominant caste re-narrativizing. When Black filmmakers are charged with telling stories of Black historical significance, they must not only capture history accurately, they must also ensure their work speaks emotionally to Black audiences. Discussing her approach to directing the 2016 film, *Selma*, director Ava Duvernay said,

> You can get caught into this thing of making a movie that's a complete tribute, and that has no resonance with people now. Yes, you're honoring these great people, but that's not what people look for in a story. They need emotional connection, and the thing that connects you emotionally are characters that you can understand. And so, we just had to get to the human element of it. That's what I knew how to do, going into the film. I know how to make films about the inner lives of people. What I didn't know how to do was to stage battles on a bridge and have 500 extras in a church . . . To me, I feel like history is a skeleton. We were just trying to put meat on the bones and fill out the lines on the page. (Collider 2014).

The job of a filmmaker is to find the story in the human elements—making history a backdrop. But histories of racism are notoriously difficult conversations to have in the American public imagination. Filmic takes of such themes can help and harm chances at fruitful dialogue. They are also burdened with presenting accurate historical representations, creating vehicles that solidify Black social identity, and convincing Hollywood that films about Black lives from Black cultural workers can be monetarily successful. I believe *Straight Outta Compton*'s success stems not just from the markers of Hollywood Representational Progress (Black cast and crew, economic success, cultural significance, and symbolic recognition) but also because of its ability to claim itself as *authentically Black* and historically accurate.

Positionality refers to the stance or positioning of the researcher in relation to the social and political context of the study—the community, the organization, or the participant group. The position adopted by a researcher affects every phase of the research process, from the way the question or problem is initially constructed, designed, and conducted. If we are to truly understand the success of *Straight Outta Compton*, we must explore the positionality of the film as a text that reflected, "all the stifling of our voices as young black people in that place at that time while a war was going on against us" (Duverney 2015) and as a product of the current moment in Black commercial cinema. In her seminal text *Contemporary African American Cinema (Framing Film)*, Sheril Antonio suggests the mid-1980s to early 2000s marked the beginning of the contemporary period of African American cinema (2002). This coincides directly with the mainstreaming of Black culture through hip-hop. As hip-hop transitioned from a genre mainly concerned with feel good tunes and intra-cultural boasts to "gangsta" rap, films about Black lives began to reflect the same. There is a vast difference between the Fat Boys' 1987 film, *Disordalies* (dir. Michael Shultz) and 1992 film, *Juice* (dir. Ernest Dickerson) in approach and theme. Black masculine performance in film mirrored the music and music videos that were saturating the market. The co-constitutive nature of film and music helped dictate the kinds of masculinity performed in life, sometimes with deadly consequences such as a circulation of the myth of the super-predator—a young Black male beyond redemption. This justification for over-policing and mass incarceration continues to haunt law and order policies. Masculinity in hip-hop, "became limited to violence and sexuality, and the emergence of the hip-hop thug was born. Films directed by young black men in the early 1990s became known as "New Black Realism" and so-called "hood films" (Boylorn 2017). Hood films were action films that paid homage to 1970's Blaxploitation tropes while embodying many of the themes evident in 1970s urban family films like the 1978 adaptation of the book, *A Hero Ain't Nothing But a Sandwich* (dir. Ralph Nelson). Urban family films were often stories about young Black (mostly male) children on the precipice of a life of crime. New Black realism cinema prided itself on its "authenticity"—if that authenticity was reflective of, "aesthetically contemporary urban settings, young black male protagonists, and an emphasis on nihilistic violence" (Boylorn 2017). This new black realism cinema was intimately entwined with "new racism," the commodification and fetishizing of markers defined as authentically Black and worthy of moral panics and state violence. Under the new racism, Black cultural texts became the containers for "class-based codes and cultural discourses [that serve] as the basis of projects of demonization against the black poor or black working-class communities" (David J. Leonard, 2006). In essence, new Black realism cinema bolstered by mainstreamed hip-hop culture shaped a new version of Black pathology in the dominate castes' imagination. At the same time, new Black realism and "hood cinema," just like hip-hop, provided a mirror for many young Black men and women that validated their understanding of their existences in under resourced communities. Like Blaxploitation cinema, hood films, "presented black men and black masculinity as invulnerable, dangerous, and endangered, within the limited confines of the(ir) ghetto" (Boylorn, 2017).

N. W. A as a rap group represented this moment in hip-hop mainstreaming and major studios funding Black films were willing to ride this wave of crossover appeal to increase their revenue. As Jaquie Jones suggests, "the industry's whole-sale investment in films that explore only ghettoes and male youth ignores the existence of a black community beyond these narrow confines—inclusive of women as valuable participants—as well as films that refuse to cater to these prescriptions" (51). The infusion of hip-hop aesthetic, themes, and sensibilities in music and film contributed directly to the invisibilization of the other half of the Black community. The female half. Much of the popularity of N. W. A. as a group existed within a cultural moment that was singularly focused on the blight of Black people—particularly those disenfranchised by the twenty-year war on poverty. The surge of new Black realism cinema such as 1991's *New Jack City* (dir. Mario Van Peeples), *Boyz in the Hood* (dir. John Singleton), and 1993's *Menace II Society,* (dir. Hughes brothers) all focused on stories of "young African Americans males coming of age in urban settings, their lives often defined by the racial dynamics and racism of the dominant culture" (Bogle 312). These stories featured undeveloped women characters who were side stories, hindrances to the protagonists, and/ or disposable sexual objects. In *Straight Outta Compton,* F. Gary Gray tried to remain true to the errors of the band and the cultural mainstreaming of hip-hop. But this text was made in 2015, not 1991. As a director, he chose not to take the opportunity to examine the misogynoir that was prevalent at that time, and in his refusal to do so, contributed to the misogynoir in the present. The success of *Straight Outta Compton* in the Black community suggests that Black audiences, enthralled by the text's "authenticity," felt little compunction to complicate N. W. A.'s misogynoir either.

BLACK AUDIENCES' COMPLEXITY

Donald Bogle says sometimes, "the most important films have not been those that the critics praised but rather those in which moviegoers found cultural signs and symbols—as well as an exploration of issues and themes and entertaining, provocative performances and concepts—with which they could identify. Often enough, very popular films have spoken to moviegoers in a far more personal way than we might have imagined. Yet other times, some of those films have moviegoers feeling frustrated—not so much just by what they said as by what they didn't say" (2016). His comments hint at the complexity of Black audiences' responses to film texts. Many scholars of Black cinema look to audiences' *cultural reception* to understand what a filmic text means for Black life at a given time. Cultural reception (Tsvian 2013) takes into consideration how audiences creatively or actively reflect on the meanings of the films, regardless of creator's expectation. Other scholars look to *Black spectatorship* (Diawara 1988), the way Black audiences have historically resisted and negotiated the ways they have been represented on the screen. Others have looked at Black spectatorship as it relates to specific types of film. For example, Jacqueline Stewart studied the way Black viewers engaged with classical Hollywood film in the past and determined Black audiences engaged in *reconstructive spectatorship*, a viewing practice that takes into consideration the myriad of ways Black spectators had to "reconstitute and assert themselves in relation to the classical cinema's racist social and textual operations" (661). Reconstructive spectatorship is also one of the few Black spectator/audience theories that considers the public aspects of spectatorship. In her assessment, viewing the text with other Black people meant their reception was shaped by the viewers' experience of inhabiting and interacting with others within the space of the theater" (662). This way of understanding takes into considerations the feeling of collectivity that occurs when watching together. The thread that links all these conceptions of Black audience response is the assumption that Black moviegoers have always known that cinema is a wholly constructed fantasy propagated by a Hollywood industry intent on monetary gain. Black audience responses are also complicated by gender and age.

Black women and girls are provided very few Hollywood texts with liberatory explorations of their complex personhood. This leaves Black female audience members tasked with reading the text against the grain. To read against the grain is to "make meanings from mainstream texts separate from the intentions of the filmmaker" (Seiter et al., 1989). This contortion in viewing practice often results in an empathetic reading, extending a level of grace to problematic text. Much of this has to do with the way film and television texts validate one's sense of belonging. Exploring Black women's positive response to Steven Spielberg's adaptation of Alice Walker's womanist novel, *The Color Purple*, Jacqueline Bobo cited Black women's reservoir of background knowledge about the conditions of Black women helped them foster a discursive reading practice of the film. The "issues that these women considered to be important were pervasive ones in Black women's lives, thus, the women could be interpellated or hailed, by a creative work in which these elements were present" (Bobo, 1993). Since there is a dearth of stories about Black women and girls told by Black women and girls in every medium (besides literature), this type of negotiated reception is inculcated in Black female life. Bobo adds, "in paying good attention to a film in which aspects of their histories were depicted, Black women were able to extract images of power and relate them to their lives" (285). Again, the convergence of history and authenticity acts as a balm against egregious narrativization. We might also turn to bell hooks' suggestion that Black women and girls often adopt an oppositional gaze as spectators of mediated text. Interrogating the gaze of black female spectators and white, mainstream cinema, bell hooks suggest, "critical black female spectators construct a theory of looking relations where the cinematic visual delight is in the pleasure of interrogation" (hooks, 2015, 1992). It would be folly to suggest all Black female spectators read visual media against the grain or find pleasure in interrogating the text. Some people sincerely want to be swept away for a few hours by watching a film. Studying gender and spectatorship in the work of Tyler Perry, Robert Patterson suggests that the "naturalization and normativization of traditional gender roles and heteronormativity contribute to the phenomena of audience members (and producers) being uncritical spectators when the foci are gender and sexuality" (26). Perhaps, what is also wrapped up in this viewing is the ride or die mythology that bears upon hip-hop and its aesthetic in music and film. Black men in hip-hop are partnered with Black women who stick by them no matter what. In *When Chicken-Heads Come Home to Roost* (2000), Joan Morgan writes,

> White girls don't call their men 'brothers' and that made their struggle enviably simpler than mine. Racism and the will to survive it creates a sense of intra-racial loyalty that makes it impossible for black women to turn our backs on black men—even in the ugliest and most sexist moments. (p. 34)

Laboring under a Black sexual politics wherein masculinity is conflated with dominance and femininity is equated with submissiveness (Collins, 2002, 2012), the misogynoir is so authentic, expected and beyond reproach that viewers fail to see it or critique it as problematic. Yet, Black women, girls and femmes are not the only audience members—Black men and boys watched *Straight Outta Compton* with pleasure. Perhaps the same logics expressed by Patterson and Collins undergird masculinist viewing practices. Studies have linked real-life performance of Black masculinity to depictions of such in hip-hop music, videos, and film. However, very few have focused on how Black men and boys negotiate or even critique sexism and misogyny in hood or hood-adjacent film.

Teens in the U.S. spend an average of more than seven hours per day onscreen media for entertainment, and tweens spend nearly five hours, a new report finds—and that doesn't include time spent using screens for school and homework (CNN 2019). Out of this screen time, adolescents spend approximately three hours per day watching film and television (Rideout 2015). For the last several years, Morgan E. Ellithorpe has done several studies on the impact of media on adolescent identity development and social identity gratification. Her studies have found that Black adolescents watch more visual media than non-Black adolescents. Black adolescents also, "seek out media messages with characters that are members of their identity groups because the characters serve as tools for identity development and social identity gratifications" (Ellithorpe, Bleakley 2016). This is especially true for Black adolescents with a strong ethnic identity. Black adolescents know when a text is targeted to them and differentiate between Black film and white film much more than white adolescents. Ellithorpe's research suggests Black young people are hungry for stories about their lives, regardless of if these stories are ripe with misogynoir.

Finally, in a study of student responses to "hood" films, Celeste Fisher found their responses to the texts were conditioned by their immediate social context (93). Factors at play in their response included who was in the room while they were viewing the work, how much of the text was misinterpreted and to some extent, their personal relationship to the conditions of the characters in the film. She notes, "response is the product not only of the individual but also of the space that he or she occupies in a particular context of interactions with others" (94). There is something to be said about watching what could be considered a problematic text in the company of others. Who wants to be the only one *not* laughing in the room?

A SPECTATOR'S PERSPECTIVE

As a Black community, we will only be able to combat misogynoir, "when we've told the truth about ourselves—[only] when we've faced the fact that we are often complicit in our oppression will we be able to take full responsibility for our lives" (Morgan, 1999). In the spirit of that charge, I will provide a brief auto-ethnography of the experience of watching *Straight Outta Compton* in the theater and then place it in conversation with the above moments of mediated discourse around the film and Black spectatorship.

I was reluctant to see *Straight Outta Compton* when it was released. As a young girl coming of age in the late 1980s to early 1990s, hip-hop was just one part of my very eclectic musical world. I enjoyed Public Enemy, A Tribe Called Quest, EPMD, Queen Latifah, L. L. Cool J, De La Soul, Erik B and Rakim, Special Ed, Big Daddy Kane, Heavy D, and the Boyz, Salt n Peppa, McLyte, Run DMC, early Tupac, and of course, N. W. A. I knew all the lyrics to "Fuck the Police" and the sequel, "Sa Prize (Part 2)." My relationship with hip-hop, specifically N. W. A., was a mixture of love and side-eye. The complicated status of being a Black feminist woman and a lover of hip-hop has been and continues to be an area of rich, intellectual engagement and outrage in my life. Every semester I screen F. Gary Gray's *Set It Off* (1995) to help my students understand intersectionality, state violence, and womanism. I wanted to see *Straight Outta Compton* to determine if it would go on the screening rotation. My reluctance came from a fear that the misogyny and violence would be too triggering, and the erasure of women in hip-hop would be too glaring. I was right, and still, I enjoyed the film. Active communal spectatorship built on kinship and the deployment of an oppositional gaze made it possible for me to find joy in a text that is rife with misogynoir.

Though it was midday in August, the movie theater was full of Black people of all ages, with the same hungry look of anticipation that comes with being given a Black film with a budget and a notable director. An enthusiastic Black audience can make even the most hackneyed script a masterpiece of entertainment. I watched and enjoyed the energetic parkour antics of Eazy-E escaping a drug bust. I slung verses with my seatmates and during the scenes depicting the making of *Fuck the Police* a Black man tapped me on the shoulder and whispered, "Damn, this song must have been your joint," and I nodded affirmatively. Kinship in the theater also meant sharing an empathetic glance with the brother to the left of me who clenched his fist and audibly inhaled at the scene where the N. W. A. members were harassed by an interracial pair of police officers. Then, the "Bye Felicia" scene happened. I watched the orgy in the hotel room with wariness and gasped when Dj Yella's sexual partner was lifted and thrown across the bed as members of the group searched for their weapons. The theater audience laughed with complete abandon. A girl who looked to be around 15 years of age said "Oops, bitch!" and laughed with her friend. I gritted my teeth and shook my head. I felt as if I was the only silent spectator. My male seatmate paid no attention to my reaction to this site of gender-based violence. As the contradictory space of hip-hop, media culture and misogynoir buttressed one another; I could not help thinking that the shrill laughter of the two young women was possibly a form of forced bravado—a desire to show that they were down. Robin M. Boylorn suggests, "a down ass chick was loyal, sexual, willing to lie, die, fight, or steal for her ni**a. She kept her mouth shut and her legs slightly open, but only for her dude" (Cooper, Morris, Boylorn 2017). Misogynoir implicates all Black and white men as well as Black and white women. The young women's laughter was a reminder that internalized misogyny begins early.

The oppositional gaze gives Black women the power to examine and challenge the white male gaze, which has enforced the ideas of white racial superiority, white supremacy, and gender inequality. hooks' oppositional gaze theory is a direct challenge to Laura Mulvey's classic feminist film theory of the male gaze where the audience is placed in the perspective of a heterosexual male and the female body is something to be looked at (objectified) and feared (controlled). According to Mulvey, the female spectator has no position. By positing that critical Black female viewers refuse to identify with white womanhood on the screen, hooks positions Black female spectators as able to deconstruct binary thinking and commit a critical inquiry of race and gender on the screen that white feminist film theorists have proven unable or unwilling to do.

As a Black female spectator committing critical inquiry of race and gender on screen, my interrogation starts with my understanding that racism is not more severe oppression than sexism. Additionally, I have always greeted the label feminist and/lesbian or queer with a nod of agreement when it has been hurled my way with the intention to insult. Finally I, like many hip-hop feminists, acknowledge finding pleasure in specific performance of masculinity—one that involves aggression, swag, and that little pelvis dip on a muscled body with developed abs. Some performances of masculinity are sexy, especially when I can clearly glean the performative aspects in the text. Take for example Gene Graham's documentary on Black strippers and their fans, *This One's for the Ladies* (2018). His look at the life of male strippers in Trenton NJ, highlights the appeal of stripper culture in the Black community as space where men and women can openly explore their sexual proclivities and identities while building fluid familial configurations. The Black male strippers and the sole Black female stripper discuss their approaches to making sexual objectification pleasurable, collaborative and fun for all, no matter how ridiculously exaggerated their performances of strength and aggression seem. The pleasure is in the fantasy and in the performativity.

Bringing my oppositional gaze to bare on *Straight Outta Compton*, I paid particular attention to what the narrative was proposing as legitimate Black masculinity. Despite all the guns under hotel beds or swagger amongst the male characters in N. W. A, the only Black man shown being violent with other Black men is the perpetual villain of hip-hop, Suge Knight. Suge Knight is portrayed as the quintessential Black Buck, a hyper-masculine Black male, often shown being violent, brutish, sexually charged, and possibly criminal. As many scholars have discussed, the Black Buck archetype has haunted representations of Black men in film from D. W. Griffith's *Birth of a Nation* (1915) to Eric Killmonger (Michael B. Jordan) in *Black Panther* (2018). This mediated depiction has had dire consequences for Black men in real life, from the lynching campaigns of the early twentieth century to the War on Drugs at the end of the twentieth century In *Straight Outta Compton*, Suge Knight's (R. Marcus Taylor) villainous masculinity is shown in direct opposition to Eazy-E and Dr. Dre, who are positioned as unwitting victims of Knight's ambitions. When Knight confronts Eazy-E about negotiating Dr. Dre out of his contract with Ruthless Records, F. Gary Gray makes a point of illustrating the size differential between Eazy-E, Knight, and his security detail. The intimidating Black men converge on the short, scrappy Eazy-E like a pack and proceed to violently assault him. As they do so, the camera backs away from the scene, never showing Eazy-E taking the blows or fighting back but making sure the audience is able to see Knight's thuggish masculinity. In a later scene, we witness Knight's pathological overreaction to having his parking place occupied. Gray intentionally shows Dr. Dre trying to intervene in the assault and being taken aback by the violence of Knight's attack. By situating the narrative of Knight's violence as an aberration, *Straight Outta Compton* effectively makes Eazy-E and Dr. Dre heroic, naïve victims, not colluders in the overall oppression of both Black men and women. This is where we circle back to the absence of scenes depicting Dr. Dre's factually accurate instances of violence against women. Misogynoir thrives in narratives where male on male violence is presented as having consequences while violence against women is dismissed as the casual norm. By not showing the "side-story" of Dee Barnes' assault by Dr. Dre, F. Gary Gray has created a film where the only legitimate violence is against men at the hands of other men and by the state.

Additionally, an oppositional reading of *Straight Outta Compton* meant walking into the theater with no expectation that its views on Black women and girls would be free of patriarchal distortion. Being a fan of N. W. A. and classic hip-hop, I was already aware of the contradictions inherent in the genre. Rap music is one of the few vehicles where Black men can express some type of emotional and psychological vulnerability, even if it is at the expense of Black women (Oware 2010). I worked extremely hard not to be unduly upset about the rampant misogyny and colorism, while also paying attention to the uses of misogyny and colorism. Interrogating the text meant bracing myself for visual harm while holding out hope that the film would be able to "reimagine male homosociality in ways that are less destructive to women" (Randolph 2018, 8). I watched for moments of resistance to the customary narratives in Black female representation but unfortunately, there were none. There is never a scene where the women in the narrative are more than nagging mothers, video-vixens, groupies, or supportive spouses whose only job is to emotionally take care of their men. Reciprocity of emotional support between the men and women in the film was not to be seen, further solidifying the text as an example of mediated misogynoir.

My experience watching *Straight Outta Compton* affirmed many aspects of discourse on Black audience and spectatorship. Though Stewart's "reconstructive spectatorship" was prompted by her investigation into classic Hollywood text, when combined with Ellithorpe's identity gratification and Fischer's group viewing findings, reconstructive spectatorship is an especially adroit tool to describe my viewing experience of this 2015 film. My interaction with other Black people in the theater did impact my experience of the film. Three components create a feeling of collective identity. For a collective identity to develop, a collective group must have continuity over time as the group attempts to adapt to its social and political environment. Secondly, the feeling of collective identity must be differentiated and distinguished with respect to other collectives. Finally, the collective must be able to recognize itself and be recognized by others (Melucci 1996). Collective identities lend themselves to the creation of in-group and out-group social identity fostered by repeated moments of identity activation. Collective identity is not only derived from the process of interaction, but from the repeated identity activations a group undergoes as it negotiates its self-identification. A Black film generally has a Black cast, a Black director and, prior to the 1990s, was targeted solely toward Black people. *Straight Outta Compton* is a Black film. Watching it, I experienced several moments where my Black racial identity was a key component of how related to the text, buttressed by viewing it with other Black people. The interaction between me and my seat mate during the writing of *Fuck the Police* scene is an especially telling moment. The face-off between N. W. A. and the interracial police officers brought up both the historical and contemporary images of police over-reach I have read about and witnessed growing up in Baltimore city. When I reacted to my seatmate's physical response to the scene, I was not met with hostility or dismissal. We had a shared moment indicative of an identity activation. For me, an identity activation was occurring when I found myself rapping the lyrics of specific songs in the film. I felt a sense of collective identity when I realized other Black people in the audience were doing the same. We were collectively having a moment that solidified feelings of group identity. In my earlier discussion of Celeste Fisher's work, I posited "who wants to be the only one not laughing in the room?" During the "Bye Felicia" scene, I literally found myself in that position. It was sobering. Though I'd steeled myself with a commitment to an oppositional gaze, warm moments of previous identity activations trumped my interrogation. Suddenly I felt like an out-group member. This leads me to believe that I did both an oppositional interrogation and a discursive reading, like Bobo's discussion of Black women's response to *The Color Purple*. As a girl who came of age during the time in which this film was set, I had adequate background knowledge of Black women and girl's experiences of hip-hop fandom to situate various scenes of misogynoir. The scenes of misogynoir felt "faithful" to the historical moment in which the film took place and as such, convergence of history and authenticity acted as a balm against egregiousness.

Media culture thrives off narratives that are familiar, replicable, and profitable. *Straight Outta Compton*'s success enriches the landscape of Black cultural production. It also helps connect young people's past struggles with state violence to our current #Movement for Black Lives. However, it does so at the expense of Black women's and girls' humanity. By erasing the consequences of gender-based violence from the narrative and adhering to an oppressive racial and color hierarchy of women's bodies, *Straight Outta Compton* misses its chance at writing a love letter to hip-hop culture that includes the women who grew up and are growing up within its contradictions.

CORRECTIVES FOR BLACK WOMEN AND GIRLS

To critique *Straight Outta Compton*'s misogynoir is not to throw it out as trash, but to do the important work of using it as a tool for changing the way we gauge Black representational progress, understand Black audience responses, and deepen our conception of what it means to represent complex Black life on screen. It is bid that we shift our focus to *broader representation* while not buying into the false ideal that increased representation is progress and progress is inevitable. In his book *Silence of Animals* (2013), philosopher John Gray defines progress as any kind of advance that's cumulative, so that what's achieved at one period is the basis for later achievement that then, over time, becomes more and more irreversible. He suggests this might be true for science and technology but is not necessarily true for politics, ethics, and civilization. The continual rollbacks of key civil rights gains (e.g., Voting Rights Act) should suffice to show progress is a myth. The debunking of the fantasy of a post-racial America through the election of Barack Obama should sober us of the notion of inevitable progress as well. Limited representation often devolves into stereotypes and archetypes, but increased visibility does not automatically mean progress. Black people can still create a myriad of narrow, flat, and unengaging Black characters. Discussing Black women in Tyler Perry films, Christopher Jacksons says, "for women in particular, their image in popular culture is a fractured one. One that is inherently contradictory, presenting misogynistic images on one hand and ideals of inequality on the other. Many images of Black women have relied on recycled stereotypes in which there is a constant assault on their womanhood" (2014, 66). Jackson is following in the footsteps of Stuart Hall's argument that "invisibility" has been replaced by a carefully regulated, segregated visibility. One can be committed to telling stories about Black women's lives while also placing them in boxes that look new from the outside but are the same on the inside. As Jackson says of Tyler Perry, "he challenges the dominant ideologies of patriarchy, but these same women end up needing men in order to find true happiness" (32). To increase diversity is to add more bodies to a media industry that is built on hegemonic cultural dominance that deploys racial logics to maintain the status quo.

To *broaden* is to widen and expand whose bodies are seen, what approaches are used to tell and distribute stories, and deepen the types of stories audiences can access. Broader representation is an ideal landscape to represent Black life. Television shows like Donald Glover's *Atlanta*, and Issa

Rae's *Insecure* are often praised as examples of progress because the Black characters are "human" and "relatable" (Harnick 2018, Stuever 2018). These terms are often code for stories with Black people who are not criminals, poor, or trying to distance themselves from criminality and poverty. These stories focus on more universal themes such as establishing a career, finding romance, and improving family life. They are less illustrations of progress than they are examples *of broader representation*. Broader representation is not solely about adding more Black people in front of and behind the camera. It is not about showcasing middle- and upper-class Black people to the erasure of the working class. It is not even about the film's crossover appeal. Broader representation means having critical and expansive depictions of the lived experiences of Black people, especially Black women and girls. I believe this can be achieved by leaning into what the filmic texts do best: help us critique ourselves and the world around us.

The lessons of stories resonate through a schema process of encoding, storing, and interpreting information. Schemas help us perceive the world and understand information. Schema theory suggests that when a message is sent and then received by the audience, the audience evaluates this message based on "direct observation, interpersonally transmitted experience, [and] and generalizations" (Axelrod 1973, 1249). Schemas can hinder our understanding of new concepts, leading us to fall back on prior knowledge rather than encouraging us to try to understand a new idea. Broader representation means creating characters and stories that do not allow folks to fall back on prior knowledge. Let's first apply broader representation to the burden of historical representation.

One of the reasons *Straight Outta Compton* was so popular was because of its seeming authenticity and historical accuracy. For me, much of that stemmed from feelings of nostalgia about the time in my life. But as Shohat and Stam make very clear, "an obsession with 'realism' casts the question [of critique] as simply one of 'errors' and 'distortions,' as if the 'truth' of a community were unproblematic, transparent, and easily accessible, and 'lies" about that community easily unmasked" (178). This idea of authenticity and historical accuracy allows audiences to ignore the fact that filmmaking is a "specific orchestration of ideological discourses and communitarian perspectives" (180). Dr. Dre and Ice Cube, the main writer/producers of *Straight Outta Compton* have moved quite far from the working-class, gangsta adjacent lives of their fictionalized characters on screen. As such, their ideological take on their culpability in the onscreen violence is self-serving. They were naive kids and Suge Knight was the bad one. But no representation on screen is safe from fallacies.

Broader representation means cultural producers create historical works that show contradictory and complex depictions of a given period rather than sanitized, self-serving narratives. This tactic in storytelling must be a collective effort that takes advantage of the changes in distribution, demographics and viewing habits of audience members to saturate the market so much so that it interrupts audience's schemas. This strategy would interrupt the feelings of nostalgia and abysmal education about history that often ignore new insights into our collective moments in time. History is created through the push and pull of multiple forces. This should be shown in filmic texts. Broader representation doesn't take away from the power of the story. To paraphrase Ava Duvernay's process of making *Selma*, when telling historical tales, cultural producers must move beyond tributes and instead create human stories of complexity that audiences can relate to emotionally. Broader representation deepens our understanding of history and complicates notions of authenticity.

Additionally, broader representation means following in the footsteps of Edward Shiappa's treatise on representational correctness by moving beyond debates over stereotypes in film. Stereotypes are unavoidable because they are simply a form of categorization that helps to simplify and systematize information. This approach does not ignore the fact that rampant stereotypes in film cause all manner of material and psychological harms to audience members in real life. What it does do is advocate for cultural producers to show characters who are adept at disidentification. Disidentification is "a survival strategy that is employed by a minority spectator to resist and confound socially prescriptive patterns of identification" (Munoz 1999, 4). People have multiple social identities with various levels of power that shift at any given moment. All social identities come with some level of stereotype that people must negotiate to be safe in the world. Broader representation means showing characters who perform, scramble, and reconstruct the "encoded messages of a cultural text in a fashion that exposes the encoded messages' universalizing and exclusionary machinations and recircuits its workings to account for, include and empower minority identities and identifications" (31). People learn how to navigate the world through mediated texts. This is especially true for Black adolescents who spend more time using media than their non-Black peers (Rideout, 2015). Black adolescents seek out Black content with Black characters that directly tackle racial themes (Ellithorpe, 2016). Disidentification relies on having a strong interior life that strives to make sense of multiple and contradictory information about the self. Black adolescents desperately need characters that have complex and rich interior lives. By showcasing characters who use disindentification as a survival strategy, such as Chiron in the 2016 Berry Jenkins film, *Moonlight,* adolescents will be able to tease out modes of being, understand better how identity is performance, and hopefully apply these strategies to their material and psychological life.

Finally, broader representation does not mean disengaging from Hollywood, regardless of its endless desire to make money by remaining risk averse in its storytelling. Regardless of if a text is produced by Hollywood or is independent, Black audiences understand films are created and distributed with the intent of securing the maximum amount of profit, and that producers will do everything in their power to recoup their money. This is merely a part of what Black people have learned to negotiate as spectators. Independent cinema is not the panacea of Black representational progress. When we elevate independent cinema over Hollywood, we ignore the fact that independent cinema can still fail to provide complex personhood to Black women and girls. Ruth Elizabeth Burke cautions against praising independent cinema as a liberatory space. She suggests this tendency, "(a) valorizes black independent films, even when they are racists, sexists, and classist; (b) fails to address the fact that a plethora of both male and female African Americans—not to mention most Americans—still shape their perceptions of themselves as well as others by what they see on Hollywood's silver screen; and (c) leaves mainstream Hollywood producers free to do what they want with the construction of our black female image" (26). In Burke's mind, a focus on independents as liberatory and Hollywood as predatory ignores the fact that both industries fail Black women and girls. I cannot agree more. As Audre Lorde says, "only within that interdependency of different strengths, acknowledged and equal, can the power to seek new ways of being in the world generate, as well as the courage and sustenance to act where there are no charters" (112). There must be a both/and approach to who gets to tell film stories and distribute them to the masses.

Broader representation means embracing the systemic shifts toward equity being put forth by the mainstream Hollywood industry, such as the new Best Picture Nomination rules created by the Academy of Arts and Motion Pictures, while continuing to place the power to make films into the hands of a broader coalition of cultural producers. F. Gary Gray, Dr. Dre and Ice Cube had a chance to tell their version of a pivotal moment in hip-hop and Black cultural mainstreaming. They used it to turn the two emcees into the heroes of an era and not critique misogynoir. Yet, its Roxane Shante's independently made biopic *Roxanne, Roxanne* (2017), eventually released on Netflix, that gets to the root of what hip-hop meant to the material lives of young, Black people. It did this by drilling down into the intimate life of one of its pioneers. Neither Hollywood produced *Straight Outta Compton* nor independently funded *Roxanne, Roxanne* are perfect storytelling vehicles. We understand the trauma of Roxanne Shante's life, but the film treats her success too casually and glosses over the predatory aspects of the music business as it relates to young, female hip-hop artists. *Straight Outta Compton* hints at but does not elaborate on the ways Dr. Dre's album, *The Chronic* served as an anthem for the April 1992, LA Riots. It missed a brilliant moment to detail how "Black anthems are dense texts that expose the negotiations at work between the West and its Others, the marketplace and the commons, and the individual and the collective" (Redman 2014, 7). By relying on both mainstream and independent cinema, audiences have the chance of experiencing rich, broad, and divergent stories of Black life.

Black independent and Hollywood filmmakers must commit to acknowledging the combination of sexism and racism fueling misogynoir and refuse to visualize Black liberation off the backs and bodies of Black women and girls. Burke contends that until that happens, "black women have little choice to deplore sexist depictions of themselves wherever they occur and to look to other sources for cinematic empowerment" (30). She suggests audience turn to independent films produced by Black feminist filmmakers and commercial Hollywood texts "produced by those who try to convey more multifaceted, depictions of black women" (30). Ruth Elizabeth Burke made these convictions in 1996. It's sobering that this call to action is still being made today.

Chapter 3

Monstrous Misogynoir

During European colonial conquest, imperialist narratives encouraged the sexual exploitation of Black women. As Shohat and Stam explains, "exoticizing and eroticizing the Third World allowed the imperial imaginary to play out its fantasies of sexual domination" (158). Due to the structural nature of these exploitative practices, Black women continue to experience disproportionate rates of sexual trauma and abuse. These traumas are undergirded by assumptions of hypersexuality which, when pitted against narratives of White female purity, often frame Black female sexuality as monstrous. Additionally, imperialist narratives included myths of African men with gigantic penises and rumors that African women engaged in sex with apes (McLinktok 2001), a key colonist trope (Shohat and Stam 1994). Unsubstantiated perceptions about Black people's sexuality were confirmed through pseudo-scientific investigation and perpetuated by scientists and politicians like Thomas Jefferson, to justify enslavement and sexual abuse. Over centuries, the perception of Black women as monstrous in body and in sexual practice has been used to justify forced sterilization (Washington 2007). The cultural creation of the monstrous Black woman has also been used to establish punitive national social welfare policies. The overly sexualized and over-productive wombs of enslaved African women haunt white narratives of Western Black female sexuality in contemporary media. Contemporary discourse about Black female sexuality is not wholly determined by colonial legacies and should not be flattened as such, however, the structures of domination that upheld these practices, namely white patriarchy and capitalism, are still at play, especially in mediated landscapes where misogynoir thrives.

BLACK HOLLYWOOD

As discussed in the previous chapter, when the entertainment industry is losing money, the distribution opportunities for Black storytelling open wide.

When white Hollywood was struggling to tell positive stories post-Nixon and governmental scandals in the 1970s, producers saw the success of independently produced Blaxploitation cinema and decided to invest in the genre (Lawrence 2016). Blaxploitation improved Hollywood's finances but "never radically upset either the racial patriarchal politics implicit in their making—the actual idea of white supremacy and patriarchy as the natural order—nor popular contemporary historical notions of race" (Dunn 2008). Blaxploitation cinema generated fantasies about Black liberation and progress while re-inscribing many colonial depictions of Black female sexuality and monstrosity. Auteurs of 1990s New Black Hollywood Renaissance were chosen to direct stories about Black people and white people's experiences, an unusual move for Hollywood (Donalson 2003). However, sustained success was out of reach for many of these directors. In a *New York Times* piece, Reggie Uguwu noted that a host of hit movies by Black directors "inspired optimism that Hollywood, despite overwhelmingly white executive leadership, had awakened to the moral and financial benefits of empowering minority artists" (2019). As the 1990s continued, "a wall was re-erected . . . and many of the same people who had been held up as the faces of a changing industry watched as their careers ground slowly to a halt" (2019). In a post-*Black Panther* (2018) and *Get Out* (2017) world, it can be argued that Black Hollywood is experiencing another renaissance due to a combination of undeniable critical box office success and the marked loss of prime-time television revenue. Additionally, the proliferation of original storytelling on streaming services such as Netflix and Amazon, as well as cable television channels including OWN and FXX, are expanding opportunities for distribution of products generated by contemporary Black Hollywood cultural producers.

The current moment in Black Hollywood has generated successful prime-time television soap operas—Shonda Rhimes' *How to Get Away with Murder* and Lee Daniels' *Empire*. Writer and producer Shonda Rhimes created her first successful television series, *Grey's Anatomy,* in 2005. Her production company, Shondaland, has produced additional hits, including the widely popular political drama *Scandal* and legal thriller *How to Get Away with Murder*, both of which are co-produced with ABC Studios. Lee Daniels is the co-creator, executive producer, and director of the television series, *Empire*, which aired on Fox from 2015–2019. A popular figure in Hollywood, Daniels also produced *Monster's Ball* in 2001 and went on to direct the 2009 film *Precious,* which received six Academy Award nominations, including Best Director. In 2013, Daniels also directed *The Butler*, a historical fiction spanning three decades in the White House.

Both *How to Get Away with Murder* and *Empire* feature strong Black female leads and consistent LGB representation. *Empire*, a soap opera based on the world of hip-hop moguls, has been praised as a drama that appeals to a spectrum of television audiences (Berg 2017), but it has also received criticism for relying on cultural stereotypes of Black Americans. Critic Mary Mitchell of the *Chicago Sun-Times wrote*, "When you throw in three scheming sons—one gay—homophobia, murder, gutter language, and explicit sex, you get what amounts to another reality TV show depicting black people behaving shamefully" (Mitchell 2015). *How to Get Away With Murder* has garnered much of the same critique, with critics pointing to explicit gay sex scenes as well as the melodramatic excess of the genre as a place for cultural concern. Of interest in both critiques is a tendency to invisibilize the importance of the racial casting to the stories. ABC executive Tony Hunt offered, "advertisers get it, and they want to draw the biggest audience possible. . . the key to Shonda Rhimes' success is her ability to create diverse shows that don't alienate any one race so that everyone can watch and engage" (Kang 2015). If we take that logic, as well as the fact that increasingly high-quality TV scripts and high salaries have lured actors of color away from movies, we have the context to discuss what a diversity of Black female representation does for contemporary mythologies of Black female sexuality. As popular culture vehicles, what types of mythologies and monstrosities do *Empire* and *How to Get Away with Murder* offer about Black women and why do these myths and monstrosities carry cultural weight?

BLACK FEMALE SEXUAL MYTHOLOGY

Popular culture is a myth-making apparatus tied to commerce and industry. It is "a theatre of popular desires, a theatre of popular fantasies . . .it is where we discover and play with identifications of ourselves" (Hall 2002). Black Widows, murderous mothers, and man-eating succubus are inspired by dreams, myths, and religious archetypes (Creed 1986). Female monsters have multiple forms: primeval mother, vampire, witch, a woman with a monstrous womb, woman as a possessed body, castrating mother, monstrous hybrid, life, and death. The monstrous-feminine emphasizes the importance of gender in constructing woman's monstrosity. Narratives of the monstrous feminine reflect male fears of the female body, its procreative power, and its potential destructiveness. Often the rhetoric of monstrosity relies on the concept of abjection: the monster is a projection of what we fear and what disgusts us. The abject figure helps define what is normative.

Patricia Hill Collins argues, "racism . . .relies. . . heavily on mass media to reproduce and disseminate the ideologies needed to justify racism. There are two themes here—the substance of racial ideologies under the new racism and the form in which these ideologies are created, circulated, and resisted"

(2005). The controlling images of the mammy, sapphire, jezebel, matriarch, and welfare queen rely on a combination of popular culture and media consumption to maintain their cultural weight. The foundation of controlling images is the control of Black women's sexuality and its procreative power. Saartjie Baartman, was a Khoisan woman from South Africa who was lured into a life of exhibitionism, prostitution, and medical slavery throughout her lifetime (Holmes 2007). Even in death, her body was used to support pseudo-science about Black women's abjection. The abject legacy of Baartman lurks beneath myths of Black women's hypersexuality. Racialized hypersexuality, "typically frames the dominant viewing public as the victim of the wanton ways of the women of color whose performance, while titillating, threatens the social fabric of white heteronormativity and public decency" (Fleetwood 2011). Still, popular culture is not static; it is always shifting and shaped by cultural mores and consumerism. When old myths of Black women's insatiable and monstrous sexuality are repackaged and presented as empowering, the forces of misogynoir rise. Male fears of the female body i.e., misogyny, lies at the center of the monstrous feminine. The intersection of the monstrous feminine and controlling images creates a monstrous misogynoir.

FAT BLACK SEXUALITY AND THE ABJECT

In popular entertainment, if a plus-sized woman is seen as sexual, it is often framed for comedic effect. This approach makes fat people's sexuality seem outlandish. Popular music and viral videos commonly present fat Black women's sexuality as hypersexual and something to be derided. For example, with its blend of hip-hop and chopped staccato beats, House music in Baltimore is known for its repetitive chants. In 2001, one of the most popular songs in the Baltimore House music scene was Diamond K's, "Watch Out For the Big Girl!" That is literally the entire lyric of the song, which was designed to invite fat Black women onto the dance floor to dance licentiously. There is a level of celebration of fat, Black female sexuality in Black culture but it is often only framed as comedic or as one-off sentimental quirky love songs, such as Anthony Hamilton's 2005 hit, "Sister Big Bone" lyrics include, "*Look like a plate of neck bones (look so good, look so good). I like to keep your body warm (uh, huh).*" Hamilton at once equates her with a plate of Southern food (neck bones) while also admiring a particular type of unabashed fat Black woman sexuality. When not framed as satire or comedy, lipoliteral readings of fat Black women often position them as asexual mammy figures or as angry, obstructionist sapphires whose pathology and unproductivity is amplified by racial stereotypes that position Blackness as abject.

Gabourey Sidibe describes herself as a "plus-sized, dark-skinned woman." As Artists and Repertoire (A&R) representative Becky on *Empire,* she maintains an affectionate and unabashedly sexual relationship with the character J-Poppa. This pairing of a larger, darker-skinned, confident woman with a rapper who sees her as sexually attractive resulted in a sex scene in Season 2's episode *A High Hope for a Low Heaven.* Lipoliteracy refers to shifting sets of cultural meanings that are attached to fat bodies (Ogdan 2013). Regardless of race, media narratives around larger bodies are often interwoven with pathology and unproductivity. Sidibe's larger, dark-skinned body, paired with her fully unapologetic appreciation of herself, runs counter to prevalent narratives about dark-skinned, plus-sized women. Though only two and a half minutes long, Sidibe's sex scene sparked several negative statements on Twitter:

RT @MissterRauy: Lawd Precious laying there like a seal washed up on
   shore #Empire
Seeing Becky on the roof had me like. . . . . .#Empire
THAT'S IT!!! I have officially had enough of #Empire
He's hitting all the walls. Becky nasty #Empire

Sidibe's acceptance of her body and her sexuality runs counter to these narratives. She responded to these critiques with aplomb. To the rampant criticism and outright horror of viewers unable to reconcile a large, dark body with sensuality, Sidibe stated:

"Also, yes. I, a plus-sized, dark-skinned woman, had a love scene on primetime television. I had the most fun ever filming that scene even though I was nervous. But I felt sexy and beautiful, and I felt like I was doing a good job."

Gabourey Sidibe's response to the backlash of monstrous misogynoir is liberatory on multiple levels. When fat people make their sexual nature visible, it creates a profound influence on wider culture (Walters 2016). Sidibe's refusal to have her body framed as abject interrupts the traditional reading of fat Black women. By asserting that she "had the most fun ever" and "felt like I was doing a good job," she wrenches fat Black sexuality out of the realms of absurdity or comedy and elevates her hard work as an actor. In declaring her nervousness, she also asserts her humanity.

Culturally, fat Black women are abjectly sexualized for daring to exist in their own skin. To be a Black and female is to embody a place of hypervisibility: at once visible and invisible, exposed and unseen. To be fat, Black, and female is to be deemed excessively accessible. Fat Black women must contend with kinesexuality, "the literal movement of fat black women's bodies that sends sexual messages to society members (fat black women included) who decode these movements into sexual and non-sexual behavior" (Patterson-Faye 2016). Viral videos of fat, Black women at events wearing high heels or Black women wearing clothing that hugs their bodies generate memes that police their sexuality regardless of the context for the wearer. Black women's sexuality framed as abject by default, so the addition of fat inserts a layer of unruly monstrosity to the reading.

OLDER BLACK FEMALE SEXUALITY AND THE ABJECT

Viola Davis plays a 50-year-old defense lawyer Annalise Keating. The character is an intelligent, dark-skinned, highly sexual woman. The impact of Viola Davis' commitment to her natural hair has made waves in Hollywood. At the 2012 Academy Awards ceremony, she appeared without straightened hair or a wig and instead sported a natural hairstyle. She continued this trend in *How to Get Away with Murder* when her character Annalise stripped off her wig to reveal her natural, short afro. This scene speaks volumes for our complicated relationship with Black female bodies as monstrous objects that defy Western standards of beauty, as well as our conception of older Black women as sexual beings. As an actor, Viola Davis' decision to reveal her natural hair on prime-time television was central to her acceptance of the role of Annalise Keating. Davis is quoted as saying,

> So, I wanted to see a real woman on TV . . . There was something for me I didn't buy about Annalise in private. It felt like who she was in private had to be diametrically opposed to who she was in public. And so, in order to do that, I felt like I had to physically take the wig off. I mean, I have no eyebrows. I have eyelashes that I put on, and there was something extremely vulnerable about that act and I know it seems like a very simple act at the end of the day but for me, that simple act really surmounted to something very powerful in the end, because what it was someone being very, very private in public, which is absolutely the cornerstone of what we do as artists. (Vulture 2015)

In her 2009 treatise on the political ramifications of Black women's hair, Althea Prince states, ". . . hair is entirely public. People can hide it on occasion, but it is always there—a symbol that is open to interpretation by others about who they deem us to be" (14). On July 3, 2019, California became the first state in the U.S. to outlaw racial discrimination based on a hairstyle. This bill was introduced in response to a viral video of a young Black/Puerto Rican male wrestler with dreadlocks who had his hair cut by a White referee during the game (Willon and Diaz 2019). In 2016, Solange Knowles released her album *A Seat at the Table*, which included a song, entitled, "Don't Touch My

Hair." She wrote it in response to regularly having her natural hair inspected by TSA when traveling. The marginalization of Black women and girls' hair has resulted in the questioning of their respectability, professionalism, political affiliation, and social class. For Black women and girls, hair politics are a battle between private and public vulnerabilities. The hair of famous Black women is read as an aesthetic signifier of their perceived (in) authentic Blackness. Natural hair, albeit afros, brains or dreadlocks are constantly entwined with ideas about Black feminist and radical politics (Sobande 2019). Historical conceptions of Black hair as unruly, untamable, and animalistic haunt depictions of Black women in mediated society. Internalized racism and idealized Western standards of beauty in Black communities have led "to an obsession with Blackgirl hair that is tamed, in order, slicked down on the sides, wrapped around in braids, or covered in girls," (Boylorn 2018). Monstrous hair mythos—from Topsy's pigtails in Harriet Beecher Stowe's *Uncle Tom's Cabin*, to Angela Davis' robust afro in the 1970s, frequently frame Black women and girls' hair as monstrous.

Over several seasons in *How to Get Away with Murder* (HTGWM), the character Annalise Keaton has been married to a white man, had an affair with a Black male police officer, and has had a sexual on-again/off-again relationship with a white woman. After the premiere of HTGWM, longtime television critic Alessandra Stanley wrote a *New York Times* piece exemplifying monstrous misogynoir, suggesting Viola Davis as "less classically beautiful" than some other, lighter-skinned black actresses" (Stanley 2014). Stanley's article reflects a double layer of abjection by pitting lighter-skinned actresses against darker-skinned actresses while positioning all Black actresses outside Western standards of beauty. She also asserted that Shonda Rhimes' autobiography should be entitled *How to Get Away with Being An Angry Black Woman*. A media storm followed, with Stanley responding that her intentions were misunderstood and blaming Twitter culture for the uproar (Sullivan 2014). Discussing her feelings about the article, Davis told *Entertainment Weekly* that "colorism and racism in this country are so powerful that the Jim Crow laws are gone, but what's left is a mindset. As an actress, I have been a great victim of that. There were a lot of things that I am that people did not allow me to be until I got the role of Annalise," (Davis 2015). She goes on to admit that prior to HTGWM, she was never sexualized and has never seen anyone like herself portrayed as such. The naked vulnerability of Annalise Keating helps to shape a counter-narrative to the Sapphire stereotype. First, by showing a 50-year-old, dark-skinned Black woman unabashedly enjoying her sexuality and a high volume of sex, HTGWM suggests older Black female sexuality is not monstrous or abject in the least. It demonstrates liberation from microaggressions and outward hostility to Black female sexuality and agency. It exemplifies an element of Black women's complex-personhood, something is rarely seen in popular media.

Across race and class, media depictions of older women who desire or pursue sex are often trivialized or treated negatively (Tally 2006), despite research that reveals, though their sexual activities may decrease, women over the age of forty remain interested in sex (Waite et al., 2009). Much of this research into the sexual habits of older women ignore Black female sexuality as a site of inquiry (Dickerson & Rousso 2009). If culture shapes the conceptions of our bodies and what they can or cannot do, then narrative depictions of older women as asexual and devoid of desire often influence how older women pursue sexual activity in real life. Recently, nighttime television shows such as Ava DuVernay's *Queen Sugar* and films such as Malcolm D. Lee's 2017 *Girls Trip*, have begun to showcase Black women over forty who desire and actively have sex. It is important to note these shows and films are often written, produced and/or directed by Black women and men.

MONSTROUS MISOGYNOIR AND
THE DECOLONIZED SCREEN

Colonization is the act of settling on and establishing control over indigenous lands and its people (Wolfe 2006). The birth of narrative cinema through D.W. Griffith's *Birth of a Nation* in 1914, coincides with the height of global imperial projects (Shobat & Stam 1994). Film and television have explicit or implicit sociopolitical aims and impact how the wider culture views and understands marginalized and colonized cultures. The scenes from *How to Get Away with Murder* and *Empire* described in this chapter offer counter-narratives to monstrous misogynoir. Lee Daniels' and Shonda Rhimes' production companies create art that Marnina Gonick calls a decolonized screen. A decolonized screen occurs when filmmakers combine the cultures of colonized or marginalized people with universal themes that all cultures experience such as birth, death, love, and loss (Gonick 2010). *Whale Rider,* the 2002 film about Maori culture, or Kasi Lemmons' take on the Southern Black family in the film *Eve's Bayou* (1997) both contain elements of magical realism that speak to larger themes of the supernatural, remembering, ancestry, trauma, and reclamation of disappeared knowledge practices. Decolonized narratives often center the colonized and marginalized as they navigate worlds made hostile by imperial conquest. Decolonizing the screen isn't solely about creating an "authentic" representation of colonized people or battling stereotypes about those people. A decolonized screen elevates the importance of placing marginalized people at the helm of each stage of production, weaving their own stories of love, life, birth, and death. Both

Empire and *How to Get Away with Murder* represent aspects of a decolonized screen because marginalized Black cultural workers have major roles in front of and behind the camera. Both texts have appealed to audiences due to their unconventional storytelling approaches and their commitment to showcasing Black cultural markers, both being critical elements of a decolonized screen.

Unlike many courtroom dramas or law procedurals, *How to Get Away with Murder* does not use racism, homophobia, sexism, and classism as superficial plot devices to artificially spike dramatic tension. Instead, the oppressions that the characters experience are grounded in their lived experiences as marginalized people. For example, in the HTGAWM Season 2 episode "It's a Trap," an older white man tells Annalise he only hired her because he believed having a woman of color represent his son would be the best way to swing the jury. He cautions her against losing by saying, "Don't give your people a bad name." Through a short flashback, this scene clarifies the rationale behind the Season 1 episode, "It's All Her Fault Pt. 2" where Keating strips off her makeup and wig, her "armor." One can assume being an intelligent, confident, assertive Black woman in a white, heterosexist, capitalist society has caused her to harden into the woman we meet in the show's premiere. Showcasing this important developmental scene helps to explain how her armor has become seemingly impenetrable. It also makes the memory of the de-armoring even more impactful. HTGAWM's temporal interruptions also help reveal how the traumas of the past lead to the high stakes' outcomes of the future.

Over episodes and seasons, HTGWM skillfully details and unfolds how racism and sexism have shaped Annalise's life. It has also shown a myriad of methods Keating has used to survive rampant misogynoir. One of the most powerful examples of her coping strategies occurs when episodes focus on the complicated relationship between Annalise and her mother, Ophelia, played by the legendary Cicely Tyson. When we are introduced to Ophelia in the season one episode, "Mama's Here Now" we watch these two dynamic Black actresses provide a master class in Black performance. The episode comes to a pivotal moment where Annalise sits on the floor between her mother's legs as Ophelia combs Annalise's hair. In a lilting Southern accent, Ophelia acknowledges the sexual abuse her daughter suffered as a child and subtly tells her about having murdered Uncle George in retaliation for the harm he caused to her child. In a 2015 *LA Times* interview between Davis and Tyson, the two actresses discuss the scene that one blogger described as "the blackest moment on TV." Tyson revels that she is often stopped by fans to talk about what that scene meant to them. Tyson is quoted as saying, "I don't know a black woman on the face of this universe that did not identify with that particular scene because that's what our mothers did with us," she said. "They snapped us between their legs and combed our hair. Any problems that existed between the two of them, they tried to work out that way" (2015). Tyson's description of Black women's responses to the scene reflects the universality and humanity integral to the decolonized screen. Through an auto-ethnography mother-daughter relationships around colorism, Kimberly Moffit notes the huge impact Black mothers have on their daughter's self-esteem and ability to survive a white supremacist culture. She says, "these systems challenge the notion of who these young black girls/ women are and, at times, (mis)treat them as 'other,' invisible, or unworthy of attention. It then becomes important during the teenage years that mothers demonstrate, unequivocally, that they support their daughters" (66). HTGWM's choice to use their text to illustrate how Black women develop communities of care moves Black motherhood from monstrous to universal.

When asked about his motivation for creating the show *Empire*, Lee Daniels said, "I wanted to make a Black *Dynasty*" (Hunt 2014). Daniels succeeded in creating a sometimes controversial but very successful late-night soap opera about a wealthy Black family in the hip-hop music industry. Columnist Mary Mitchell of the *Chicago-Sun Times* wrote, "When you throw in three scheming sons, one gay, homophobia, murder, gutter language, and explicit sex, you get what amounts to another reality TV show depicting black people behaving shamefully," (Kang 2014). In *Empire*'s six-season prime-time television run, the drama complicated conventional depictions of the Black family, Black wealth, and Black cultural mores. One of the distinct elements of the decolonized screen is its celebration and reverence for the cultural markers of marginalized people. *Empire*'s set decorator, Caroline Perzan, adorned the walls in Lucious and Cookie Lyon's upscale home and studio with art by Black visual artists, including Kehinde Wiley, Kerry James Marshall, and Barkley L. Hendricks. By showcasing the work of Black visual artists, *Empire* pivoted away from Eurocentrism and expanded notions and representations of fine art.

As examples of a decolonized screen, *Empire* and *How to Get Away with Murder* have pushed back against colonial narratives of monstrosity that prime Black women for exploitation and negative life outcomes. Gabourey Sidibe, a dark-skinned, plus-sized actress and Viola Davis, a darker-skinned, older actress represent a segment of the Black female population that is rarely afforded full, complex, and healthy sexuality on screen. Cultural texts such as *Empire* and *How to Get Away with Murder* can intervene in narratives of Black women and girls by affording them the complexity and humanity they deserve. Let's hope this trend continues.

Chapter 4

Surviving Misogynoir

The R. Kelly Fallout

When I was 13, I met two of my friends in downtown Baltimore to see a horror movie. After the movie, we separated to head to our individual bus stops. Downtown Baltimore on Sundays in the late afternoon is relatively sleepy, as most businesses shuttered by 6:00 pm and tourists and workers filtered away from the Inner Harbor's shops and restaurants. My bus stop was located at City Hall and directly across the street from the Baltimore City Police Department Headquarters. I was the sole person waiting for the bus in my long winter coat, a pair of boots, jeans, and a knit hat. As I waited, I noticed a sedan with tinted windows driving slowly toward me. I paid little attention at first, but I then noticed it had circled the block and was once again driving very slowly past my stop. My bus was running late, and the reality of being 13 years old on the corner of a deserted and darkening bus stop filled me with fear. The sedan with tinted windows rolled past me for the third time, this time slowing to a crawl. The car sped up and made a right as if to circle the block again. At that moment, a squad car drove toward me and feeling great relief, I waved it over. The police officers lowered the windows. As I peered in, I noticed one officer was Black, the other was white. I told them that a sedan was circling the block in a threatening manner and asked if they would wait nearby until the bus arrived. They looked unconcerned. The Black officer asked me, "How much are you selling it for?"

At first, I didn't understand his question and I answered, "What?" The white officer responded, "How much are you selling it for?" I was taken aback and immediately said, "I am 13 years old!" To which the Black officer responded, "We've seen 'em younger." In shock, I had no idea how to respond. At that silent moment, the city bus arrived, and I leapt on, spilling my sweaty coins on the ground. After organizing my fare and myself, I walked to the back of the bus, careful to avoid eye contact with every adult. I sat in the back of the bus and tried not to cry from embarrassment and shame I know now was not mine to carry.

Fast. Ass. Girls. These three words haunt many young Black girls' understanding of their sexuality, their sexual agency, and consent. On July 28, 2018, Kiki (Cleo J) of the website the Uppity Negress posted *An Ode to Fast Ass Girls* on the website Medium. Below is an excerpt:

> An Ode to "Fast Ass Girls,
> Who will be blamed for being born female in this world,
> That views them as consumable first and human second.
> An Ode to the "Fast Ass Girls
> Who were slut shamed before they knew what sex was?
> Or what a Vagina Does,
> . . . Because Grown Ass men were checkin. . . for her.
> An Ode to the "fast ass girls"
> Who were cat called before puberty because
> Grown men felt like they could take liberties when you were walking
>   alone.
> An Ode to the "fast ass girls
> Who didn't feel safe to tell her momma her "man" was inappropriate
> Way before she told you to cover up when he was "home"
> An Ode to the "fast ass girls"
> Who's momma tried to beat the "slut" out of her body
> Who's resentment festered in her bruises, a lobby,
> A powder keg seeking love.
> An Ode to those "fast ass girls"
> Who never felt safe at home
> Because they wanted love and protection
> And only got shame, fear, rejection, and broken bones.
> An ode to fast ass girls
> Who turned to the streets to fill their voids
> And found that the world was an unkind place if you had a void
> between your legs

Kiki's ode captures many of the themes central to the adultification of Black girls. Being seen as sexual objects to be consumed before they even understand sex and sexuality; having to learn how to deflect street harassment before puberty; navigating the sexual objectification of older men, boys, and family members; negotiating ones' burgeoning sexual awakening while navigating the insecurities of the older women in their lives; the blame and abuse thrust upon them simply for existing. The discourse in Kiki's poem to fast ass girls is exemplified in dream hampton's 2019 Lifetime documentary, *Surviving R.*

Kelly. This six-part series documented the R&B artist's decades-long sexual abuse of Black women and girls, exploring the legacy of collusion and protection that allowed the abuse to continue. During the week of airing, the Rape, Abuse & Incest Network (RAINN) reported a twenty-seven percent increase in calls (Shugerman 2019). dream hampton's investigation sparked robust dialogue throughout Black communities, on social media, radio, and news programming. For example, in my natural hair salon, I argued with several women who blamed R. Kelly's victims for their own victimization. While each of them condemned R. Kelly for being an abuser, they also critiqued the abused girls' parents who accepted money to stay quiet about the abuse, and they referred to the victims as "fast ass girls."

In July 2017, the resurgence of new sexual abuse allegations against R. Kelly prompted Atlanta Arts Administrator, Oronike Odeleye to act and start a petition to take R. Kelly's music from Atlanta airwaves. Her continued efforts have been bolstered by the #MeToo movement. #MeToo was started by Tarana Burke in 2007 as a call to action for Black women and girls experiencing gender-based violence. In 2017, the movement took on a new life as a call to action from US celebrities who have experienced gender-based violence. Since the documentary aired, R. Kelly has been dropped from his Sony record contract and several former celebrity collaborators have made statements distancing themselves from the artist (Nilles 2019). In September 2021, R. Kelly was found guilty on four counts of producing child pornography and five counts of enticement of a minor to engage in criminal sexual acts, sexual exploitation of children, forced labor, and kidnapping (Chow and Bates 2019). The fallout from *Surviving R. Kelly* has been so widespread that it prompted Lifetime to create a follow-up special, *Surviving R. Kelly: The Impact*, which aired May 4, 2019. Through a textual analysis of dream hampton's *Surviving R. Kelly*, this chapter explores the ways internalized misogynoir fosters a culture of silence, blame, judgment, and dismissal of sexual abuse within Black families and communities. I refer to R. Kelly's inner circle as a family in reference to a history of Black kinship in the United States that has been complicated by the socio-historical fact of enslavement and U.S. policies, such as mass incarceration, that have produced fractured Black families. For Black people, identification with a kin group is "a major aspect of identity from birth" (Stewart 2007). During enslavement, Black people were deemed property and were excluded from the right to create families. After the Civil War, Black families sought to create family units by locating their blood kin, legally marrying, and through childbirth/adoption and inheritance practices. Today, economic constraints, migration, disproportionate incarceration, and extended kinship circles shape and weave Black family units in complex ways that are not always tied to blood relationships.

As Pearl Stewart reports in her ethnography of Black families and kinship, "participation in extended kinship or family networks has been important to the survival and/or advancement of African Americans. African Americans continue to exist within the context of the extended family structure rather than as discrete units despite the influence of the larger society" (2007). R. Kelly's large network of economic dependents, blood kin, personal assistants, industry executives, and artists/performers interviewed in *Surviving R. Kelly* all represent an extended family unit and operated as such to silence victims of sexual abuse.

The secrecy that obscures and embeds familial sexual abuse owes its legacy to the impact that "slavery and systemic racism [has had] on our family dynamics, and how the still-pervasive fear of institutional racism and its agents keep our families from reporting abuse to the authorities" (Stone 2004). Studies have shown that Black girls are more often abused by relatives other than their fathers than white girls. There is a 22 percent probability that Black women will be raped over the span of their lifetimes (Stone 2004). Studies investigating the economic cost of rape in the U.S show a population economic burden of 3.1 trillion dollars over the lifetime of rape victims. These costs encompass, "short and long-term physical and mental health treatment, lost work productivity, criminal justice costs, and property loss" (Burke 2017). In her therapeutic memoir, *No Secrets, No Lies*, Robin Stone identifies four "ripple effects" from the experience of child sexual abuse within families.

> 1) Children often do not reveal they have been abused; they show it through their behaviors (withdrawal, bed-wetting, trouble in school, and sudden spiked interest in sex). 2) Siblings of survivors 'often carry the knowledge that a sister or brother is victimized and lives with the fear that they could be next' (55); or the sibling is forced to choose sides. 3) Spouses/partners of abusers may dismiss or ignore suspicions of child sexual abuse to protect their spouse/partner, while parents of sibling abusers are torn between loyalty to the abuser-child and their victim-child. 4) Extended family members might 'struggle with guilt by association' due to their lack of intervention or active efforts to protect the family abuser. (55)

A NORM OF SILENCE

Nancy Boyd-Franklin suggests that woven within the dance of family sexual abuse is the notion that the abuse is an "open secret"—something that is generally known but not discussed, or it is an active deception—a willful obfuscation of known events. Social identity is a person's sense of who they are based on their group membership. The group to which one belongs is an important source of pride and self-esteem and gives one a unique sense of belonging to a specific social order—the specific arrangement and norms of the kinship group. Family sexual abuse can be devastating across generations. "The keepers of social secrets must have a very good reason for maintaining secrecy; the threat . . . extends beyond the individual interests of the survivors, constituting a threat to the entire social order" (Tener 2017). Choosing not to "air dirty laundry" or "put ones' business out in the street" has to do with an aversion to disruption of the social order, the perpetuation of respectability politics, fear of state intervention, economic precarity, and, I argue, internalized misogynoir, within Black kinship groups.

In the first episode, "The Pied Piper of R & B" dream hampton showcases the childhood and family history of R. Kelly and illustrates his rise to fame. Of note in this episode is the revelation that not only did R. Kelly experience childhood sexual abuse between the ages of 7–14, but his younger brother Carey was also sexually abused. In the documentary, Carey Kelly discusses an interview between R. Kelly and Tavis Smiley where R. Kelly reveals that he was sexually molested. R. Kelly tells Smiley,

> Well, um, I'm not gonna throw any of my people or my family under a bus, but I feel I owe my fans, um at least enough for them to have an understanding as to what I went through. I was molested when I was seven and, yes on to maybe 13, 14, something like that, uh, by people in my family. Sexually, it woke up my hormones a lot earlier than they were supposed to be awakened. (2012)

R. Kelly's assertion that he was not going to "throw any of my people or my family under a bus" exemplifies the artist's belief in family wholeness. It also reveals his fear that full disclosure would disrupt the social order of his family. His response provides some insight into his concept of family as a place where secrets are kept and where disclosure is positioned as disloyalty. The fear of family disloyalty is also influenced by decades of pseudo-science and policies that have positioned the Black family as abnormal and dysfunctional. Disclosure would invite outside scrutiny that would tarnish the family's image. Following this revelation, Carey Kelly said,

> I don't think that he's lying. Because it happened to me. You know, I really don't talk to people about a lot of things that I have been going through. I just I just keep it and hold it. I was molested by a family member, and that shook my world, you know, 'cause I-I didn't understand it. Um, I knew it wasn't right, even though I was six years old at that time. I knew it wasn't right, but it was happening to me. I was afraid to tell my mom, um, um, because of the person, who was there. I-I didn't I didn't know if she was gonna believe me, so I was afraid to tell her.

Robert, him being my big brother, I brought that to him and told-told him what happened to me. And when I told him what happened to me, um he didn't, he didn't really respond to it like I felt that he should.

When I told him, he said, 'No, that didn't, that didn't happen, that didn't happen to you.' And I said, 'Yes, it did.' 'You know,' Robert said, "No, it didn't.' Then I left it alone. I really knew not to take it to my mom then. My brothers was the test. If they believed me, then maybe I could've took it to an adult.

Using his older brother as a "test case," Carey Kelly's attempt at disclosure was met with gaslighting, a "form of psychological manipulation in which a person seeks to sow seeds of doubt . . . making them question their own memory, perception and sanity" (Stern 2007). Childhood sexual abuse is complicated by the fact that it often leaves little bodily harm, making it harder for survivors to "label their experiences as abuse" (Stone 39). The Kelly brothers' joint confessions demonstrate that they grew up in a household where personal safety was not to be expected. R. Kelly claims his sexual abuse "woke up [his] hormones earlier than they were supposed to be awakened," which made him curious about sex at an early age. When asked if he ever talked about his hardships as a child, his music teacher Dr. Lena McLin reported that although he didn't talk about his experience of abuse, "you knew about it, because it came out in the music in what they express, you know. Children express what they fear, they love, that's around them, you know. And he was very, very, aggressive." Dr. McLin's reaction supports the findings of scholars of childhood sexual abuse who claim children do not disclose their abuse, but they do show evidence in their behavior. Multiple sources in the documentary claim that once R. Kelly had music as an outlet for expression, his entire demeanor shifted from being a shy, isolated child who could not read to being overly confident and sexually aggressive. Discussing Black male sexuality, bell hooks claims, "sexuality is the primary place where [Black men] are told they will find fulfillment. No matter the daily assaults on their manhood that wound and cripple, the black male is encouraged to believe that sex and sexual healing will assuage his pain (69). hooks believes aggressive sexual acts by Black men are an attempt to gain power within a system that disempowers. Although the system to which hooks refers is the white, hetero-patriarchal landscape, I believe her assessment can also be applied to more insular systems. As Candice Norcott states in *Surviving R. Kelly,* "Child sexual abuse confuses power and control with sex. And so children may want to say, like, 'I want to be the one that's in that power position,' right? 'I never want to be a victim again. I want to be the person that's in the power in a sexual relationship.'" By showcasing the childhood sexual abuse in R. Kelly's family of origin, *Surviving R. Kelly* provides a blueprint for further discussion of the child sexual abuse that grew over three decades of R. Kelly's stardom.

MISOGYNOIR & CARING ABOUT BLACK GIRLS

In discussing R. Kelly's proclivity for hunting potential victims at local malls, one interviewee stated, "people will say, 'well, why didn't anyone notice?' The answer is that we all noticed; no one cared because we were black girls." This statement points to the larger issue of misogynoir undergirding the legacy of childhood sexual abuse revealed in the documentary. Four assertions of misogyny and racism support the belief that "no one cared" about Black girls. The first is the historical legacy of hypersexuality and sexual violence in Black women and girls' lives. The second is the invisibilization of Black women and girls in anti-rape rhetoric. The third issue is the tendency to place Black women's and girls' liberation secondary to Black men's victimhood status. The final fact is the very real power of the entertainment industry which uses media culture and spectacle to profit from harming Black women and girls.

Scholars have charted and theorized about Black female sexuality and sexual violence from several different disciplines. All agree that since the days of colonial conquest, the hypersexualization of Black women and girls has equated Black female sexuality with promiscuity and availability. The stereotype that Black women and girls are always ready for sex anytime, anywhere, and with anyone haunts the popular imagination, impacts Black women's and girls' reproductive health, and increases their contact with the carceral system. For centuries, Black women and girls were literally viewed as unrapeable. It wasn't until 1861 that a Black woman could file a rape charge against a white man (Bishop 2018). Whites wishing to reclaim and maintain racial dominance used rape as a weapon of terror post-Reconstruction through the Civil Rights era. The temperance and suffrage movement of the late 1800s "raised the legal age of consent to from 10 to 14–18 depending on the state." In 1895 a Kentucky legislator argued, "I regard the 12-year-old girl as being capable of resisting the wiles of the seducer as any older woman" (Shuy 2012, 5). This comment is striking in its similarity to the 2002 response of the jury in Chicago that failed to convict R. Kelly of sexual misconduct with a 13-year-old. During this time, jurors literally claimed, "It seemed like the girl on the tape was much more developed" (St. Clair and Ataiyero, 2008). Historically, rape was not only used to subjugate Black women and girls. The accusation of Black male sexual assaults on white women justified the lynching of over 4,715 Black men between 1882–1946 (Wriggens 1983). Rape continues to be used as a tool of "coercion, control, and harassment" (McGuire 2010). In our heteropatriarchal society, myths of Black female hypersexuality paired with laws and policies that are unevenly applied to Black lives in the U.S. effectively strip Black women and girls of victimhood status.

The anti-rape movement owes much of its legacy to the activism, organizing, and storytelling of Black women and girls' experiences of sexual violence (McGuire 2010), but Black women and girls are largely excluded from narratives of anti-rape activism. Anti-rape discourses and research have been theorized through a lens in which "women" is synonymous with white women (Dougherty and Calafell 2018). Media images of the sexual violation of Black women are often only shown in the context of prostitution or domestic abuse perpetrated by Black men. White women, on the other hand, are subject to a myriad of sexual abuse scenarios in media culture. including domestic violence incidents and stranger rape victimization. As scolding, judgmental, and sexist the portrayals of victimized white women may be, white female experiences are most often the only ones that are documented, reproduced, and advocated against by mainstream media, mainstream feminism, and neoliberal punitive practices. Feminist advocacy against rape has increased crime control measures bolstered by the neoliberal turn to the state as the enforcer of normal family values. Gillian Harkins points out that "governmental apparatuses tend to use statistics about violence against women of color to ground legislation fundamentally oriented to protecting white women" (2011, ch.3). Yet, the testimony and advocacy of heroines such as Recy Taylor and Fannie Lou Hamer, are rarely cited as impactful. For example, in August 1974 the rape of Joan Little, an imprisoned Black woman, by a guard at the jail in Beaufort County, NC, galvanized public focus on the terror of rape. The white jailer, Clarence Alligood, attacked Joan Little in the Beaufort County Jail. Joan killed Alligood with an ice pick he had taken into her cell, and then escaped from jail. Little was caught and charged with murder. Activists, including Angela Davis, led the national outcry for justice for Joan Little. Eventually, a jury acquitted Little of the killing. High profile rape cases such as these (McGuire 2010) gave hope that groups of committed citizens can fight against injustice and institutionalized violence and obtain equal rights. Another example of white women's victimization being foregrounded at the expense of women of color's victimization and activism the initial crediting of actress Alyssa Milano as the creator of #MeToo in 2017 when it was Tarana Burke, a Black female activist who started the #MeToo conversation ten years prior. #MeToo may have influenced the reception of the *Surviving R. Kelly* documentary, but it was the work of #MuteRKelly, created by a Black woman that kept R. Kelly's predatory behavior in the spotlight. If Black women's and girls' activism is not acknowledged as central to the anti-rape movement, not only are their claims of victimhood status ignored, so are the unique confluences of racism and sexism erased from anti-rape legal and policy advocacy.

The notion that "no one cared because it was Black girls" also exists because the needs of Black women and girls are often trumped and obscured by the rhetoric of Black liberation in which Black is synonymous with male. Both Black men and women in the United States experience gendered oppression. An example of this is the neoliberal restructuring of welfare. Welfare, primarily seen as benefiting lower-economic class Black people, was transformed in the 1990s to "workfare" under an ideology that framed Black women as, "abnormal, truncated, suspect beings who threaten the moral order" (Wacquant 2009, ch.3). Black men, on the other hand, are trapped in neoliberal punitive policies that have resulted in increased incarceration in U.S. jails. Although both groups experience victimization under racism, it is often argued that Black men are the more vulnerable population. David Carbado believes "black men occupy a privileged victim status in antiracist discourse." This is quite apparent in the antiracist discourse about crime and in antiracist responses to domestic abuse. Much antiracist discourse tends to reveal the extent to which Black men are victims of "a racist criminal justice system" (2005, 2). This rhetoric becomes vividly apparent in contemporary conversations about Black male victimization and sexual assault allegations. Clarence Thomas' response that Anita Hill's accusation of his sexual harassment and the subsequent media fallout was the equivalent of a "high-tech lynching" was an attempt to use the history of racial terror experienced by Black men as a deflection from accusations of impropriety. The rhetorical defenses continue to occur when Black men are accused of sexual violence by Black women. As Britney Cooper aptly states, "to deal with Black women's struggles would be to have to confront issues of male privilege, rampant sexism, and copious amounts of sexual and physical violence [that is] perpetrated on Black women at the hands of Black men" (Cooper 2017). When accusations are hurled at Black men, rhetoric about the disenfranchisement of Black men is often the response. Historically, Black women have been tasked with "uplifting the race," which has often been code for uplifting the Black man at Black women's expense. David Carbado discusses this in his critique of domestic violence advocacy in the Black community, noting, "there is political currency in the 'endangered Black male' trope, which, when invoked in the context of domestic abuse, pits Black men's interest in avoiding the consequences of being prosecuted by a 'racist criminal justice system' against Black women's interest in being free from Black male sexual and physical violence" (Carbado 2005, 2).

Media culture reinforces norming behaviors, disseminates information, and acts as a vehicle for understanding individuals and communities. It is a driving force of economic production, creating and determining the global market. As media culture has expanded exponentially over time, so has the nature of mass media spectacle. Movies, television, social media, and music platforms require uniformity in messaging to maintain cultural relevance. There are uneasy alliances between R&B and hip-hop artists and the industry that promotes aggressive and violent conceptions of male sexuality and masculinity. Here again is evidence of Black men's embraceability and un-embraceability. When a Black male celebrity's sex life is subject to spectacularized media culture, these oppressive stereotypes can also be leveraged, marketed, and made profitable by the neoliberal cultural industry, ignoring social critique that could allow space for the real exploration of Black male sexual experience. *Surviving R. Kelly* illustrates how R. Kelly became more profitable as an entertainer as allegations of his sexual impropriety surfaced. The documentary shows a clip of a BET interview with R. Kelly and Aaliyah where they are asked directly about their relationship. R. Kelly responds, "Let's just get the record straight. We're just very close" to which Aaliyah adds, "He's my best friend." R. Kelly and his network promoted a culture where direct questions about their relationship were deflected but teased to grow audiences and increase record sales. In the documentary, Leslie "Big Lez" Segar suggests the mystery was simply a part of Kelly's self-promotion strategy.

Media critics discuss the consequences of the tape that showed R. Kelly raping a 13-year-old, highlighting the spectacle it generated and what it did for R. Kelly's public image. The tape was spoofed in pop culture texts from *South Park* to *Chappelle's Show*. After Kelly survived his trial, he went on to still make light of his proclivities. When music journalist Toure later asked Kelly if he like teenaged girls, Kelly responded, "When you say 'teenage,' how old are we talking?." These kinds of deflections contributed to R. Kelly's image as an anti-hero.

Surviving R. Kelly exposes the way the singer made a career out of toeing the line between embraceable and repellent. As R&B/Hip-Hop has become more and more profitable, its image has embraced old tropes of hypersexuality and reinforced the patriarchal domination of Black women. Aime Ellis describes today's R&B/Hip-Hop landscape as one where the Black male body has come to signify "both literally and figuratively the convergence of death and desire in contemporary U.S. popular culture" (Ellis 3). In music videos, male and female performers show more skin, are more explicit about sex in their songs, and their bodies are increasingly fetishized. Black male bodies and sexuality are determined by the market. According to Cassandra Jackson, the sexualized thug is both intimidating and titillating, playing on "dialects of white fear and fascination" (2011, 49). Considering R. Kelly an anti-hero is not only about white fear and fascination—but it is also about Black willingness to embrace modes of violence against Black women and girls at the hands of Black men. This love/hate relationship with thug sexuality is reflected in an "economy in which [black men] are imagined and imagine themselves as at once desired and under siege, the procreative symbol of life itself and yet facing the imminent threat of death" (Ellis 8). This imaging is fueled by the marketing of Black male bodies and can be seen as an example of the use of Black male bio-power, one that benefits them economically but also "disciplines the body into perversely panoptic obedience" (Ellis 11). Compulsive sex can be viewed as a way of exerting power when one is powerless in the panoptical gaze. Black artists who profit from compulsive sexual imagery are retaining some forms of power, but that power can only work in ways that support the images deemed acceptable by the neoliberal media culture industry. Black celebrities are often held up as examples of racial progress. At the height of his popularity, R. Kelly was simultaneously celebrated and problematic He used his own controversy fomented by the neoliberal media culture industry to propel him forward and evade consequences for his abuses. According to one interviewee, "Kelly created and occupied a position of outrageousness that kind of masked everything that was happening behind the scenes" (Hampton 2019). The familiar rhetoric of "trying to bring a Black man down" surfaced in his defense. It's always sobering that that defense is often made on the bruised backs of Black women and girls—illustrating a cultural commitment to misogynoir. A norm of silence, blame, judgment, and dismissal contributed to the creation of a world where a famous Black male R&B singer could openly prey on Black girls for over thirty years and suffer no consequences.

The Waltz

Incest is a threat to the social order of a family. Since the 1980s narratives of childhood sexual abuse and incest have become commonplace in the cultural milieu, recovering the hidden realities of violence against women and children. Narratives of sexual violence also "lend itself to new hegemonic forms of domestic consumption" (Harkins 2009). Stories of childhood sexual abuse have helped liberate survivors while also creating an industry of consumption. Amid this liberation/consumptive space, the stories of the victims of R. Kelly's abuses were largely obscured until *Surviving R. Kelly* aired. The misogynoir inherent in these stories of childhood sexual abuse is a mix of carefully choreographed silence, blame, judgment, and dismissal.

SILENCE

Throughout *Surviving R. Kelly*, the word family is frequently used when discussing R. Kelly's network of performers, managers, assistants, and executives. Each of his victims felt uniquely connected to R. Kelly and to one another, like siblings and close cousins. In families where child sexual abuse occurs, silence is paramount to maintaining the social order. This becomes complicated when predatory acts are exposed to the entire family and can no longer be categorically denied. Jovante Cunningham recounts the family secret involving Aaliyah, revealing in the midst of a prank on the tour bus, a door opened and revealed Kelly having sex with Aaliyah. She says, "[a]fter that, it kind of started the breakup of everything and everybody . . . Our whole family just kind of ripped up." The trust necessary to maintain R. Kelly's entertainment family was destroyed with this revelation. Family trust was further corrupted when R. Kelly married underage Aaliyah. When Kelly told Demitrius Smith about Aaliyah's pregnancy, and asked to witness their marriage, Smith reports, "I was so disappointed in him, 'cause I really believed him when he said that, you know, he wasn't doing and messing with Aaliyah." Demetrius' disappointment illustrates the feeling of family destruction that came from witnessing the relationship between R. Kelly and Aaliyah even though earlier in the documentary, he willingly facilitated R. Kelly's habit of visiting the local schools and malls to find young women to bring into the fold.

In the documentary, the female singers within R. Kelly's entertainment orbit, all between 14–17 years old, talked about the fun, sisterly atmosphere they shared with one another. That they did not see a problem with fraternizing with an older man speaks to a willful obfuscation of the realities of their family dynamic. This is also evident in the language Demetrius uses to describe R. Kelly and Aaliyah's relationship. He says, "I really believed him when he said that, you know, he wasn't doing and messing with Aaliyah." Referring to sex and impregnation of a minor as "messing with" obscures the highly problematic situation. Society's narratives of sexual violence often focus on violent stranger attacks, not broken trust amongst a family unit. If a victim does not have bruises or scars, or if the abuse is positioned as a normative part of the family dynamic, "it can be difficult to see that a deliberate crossing of the boundaries of appropriate behavior is indeed a form of violence" (Stone 2002, 55).

BLAME

Scholars of child sexual abuse identify those personal and interpersonal factors inhibit disclosure of abuse in families. Personal factors include feelings of shame, responsibility, and fear of the consequences to one's personal livelihood and safety. Interpersonal factors include fear of social isolation from the group, broken communication systems with the family and lack of trust amongst the group (Tener 2017). Victims of sexual abuse often blame themselves for what they "allowed" to happen. Undergirding blame are feelings rooted in shame, which is further compounded by internalized misogynoir. Black women and girls are relational, as such, a sense of pride in identity stems from validation by others within the group. Shame manifests on a personal level when one feels that the group will negatively view their actions. Shame "extends beyond a single incident and becomes an evaluation of the self" (Harris-Perry 2010, 104). Shame also shrinks one's sense of self, leading to self-isolation from the group. The victim-survivors in *Surviving R. Kelly* illustrate many of these concepts in their retelling of events.

Jovante Cunningham was 14 years old when she became a member of R. Kelly's entertainment family. She wanted to become a professional singer and believed R. Kelly when he told her he would help her with her career. Membership in R. Kelly's entertainment family resulted in years of sexual abuse and social isolation. What is telling in her narrative is upon engaging with R. Kelly, she did not remember Kelly asking her age at any point. Jovante met R. Kelly in 1991 and yet, thirty-eight years later, she still places the onus of verifying R. Kelly's age on herself and not the man who sexually abused her. Cunningham also invokes self-blame as she tells of her role in recruiting young girls into R. Kelly's family. She discusses hearing rumors of Kelly's behavior and being coerced to recruit other young girls into the family, never linking it to sexual abuse.

R. Kelly's former singer and collaborator, Stephanie "Sparkle" Edwards, introduced R. Kelly to her 12-year-old niece who aspired to be a rapper. Her niece would later be implicated in the 2002 R. Kelly sex tape scandal. In the interview, Edwards describes arriving at the studio to record and finding her niece alone, despite the fact that her family was strict about adult/child interactions. In *Surviving R. Kelly*, R. Kelly's female victims describe themselves as "naïve," "young," and "easily influenced." Adolescents are young, easily influenced, and impulsive but in the context of *Surviving R. Kelly*, these girls' feelings of internalized shame deflect blame from the predator, R. Kelly. Misogynoir leads Black women and girls to feel ashamed of their sexuality and sexual abuse. The documentary provides startling evidence of this in the interview of an older, white male juror from R. Kelly's child pornography trial. The juror, John Patrean, admits to acquitting R. Kelly because, "I just didn't believe them—the women. I know it sounds ridiculous. The way they dress, the way they act. I didn't like them. I voted against them. I disregarded all what they said."

This juror's bias is based on a combination of racism, classism, and sexism. In his response his disdain for the Black women witnesses is clear. This cycle of logic is evidenced in the story told by Jerhonda Pace, who met R. Kelly after his child pornography trial. A self-described "superfan," she was 14 years old when she first began sneaking out of the house to attend the trial. During the trial, R. Kelly gave Pace his contact information and began communicating. After he was acquitted, R. Kelly contacted Pace and invited her to his home. After they shared stories about their respective childhood sexual abuse, R. Kelly asked her to model her swimsuit for him. Before their first sexual encounter she told him she was a virgin, Kelly said it was perfect because, "'I get to train you and I get to take your virginity'." She then admits Kelly did not ask her age until after they'd completed oral sex. He then encouraged her to lie about her age to others. Pace was raped, even though Pace never used the term "rape" to describe what happened to her. In the documentary, a significant amount of time is devoted to the monetary payoffs and payouts R. Kelly made to his victims to maintain their silence. Even his illegal marriage to Aaliyah is overshadowed by the money he gave to her parents upon the annulment of their marriage. The discourse around making fiscal amends to the people R. Kelly harmed is complicated by the fictive kinships tying Black American identities together regardless of a blood connection. Every woman who has accused R. Kelly has suffered in the court of Black public opinion.

Stephanie "Sparkle" Edwards discussed how testifying against R. Kelly during the child pornography trial ruined her relationship with her family, stating, "I don't know what my family was thinking. As I said, we were estranged. For ten years I didn't speak to my family because of that (bleep). It's crazy." DJ Kanika "Kitti" Jones similarly feared judgment from her family, adding, "[f]ear of judgment becomes a powerful deterrent of self-advocacy."

DISMISSAL

The myth of Black female stoicism and strength contributes to a culture where Black women's and girls' gender-based trauma is readily dismissed. The casual acknowledgment of the uncle, cousin, father, family friend, and grandfather who sexually abuses female family members not only normalizes deviant behavior, but it also makes the aftermath the survivors' cross to bear. Robin Boylorn asserts "there has to be a way to be okay without having to be so damn strong" (118). *Surviving R. Kelly* outlines away by acknowledging and elevating the emotional fluidity of Black women and girls. There are tears, there is cursing, there is mascara running down cheeks. I believe this is one of the reasons why *Surviving R. Kelly* has garnered wide cultural attention. Rarely are there tales of Black female victimhood that stray from the narrative of Black women's and girls' superhuman emotional strength. Women and girls in the documentary are allowed to be vulnerable, complicated, and not tied to respectability politics. Lisa Van Allen's frank discussion of her sexual encounters with R. Kelly is straightforward and clear. She is not embarrassed when recounting instances of performing oral sex or having oral sex performed on her. Her focus is on the abuse R. Kelly predicated upon her. The documentary's illustration of the struggles of the parents who are actively trying to recover their daughters from R. Kelly's circle focuses on emotionality, not spectacle.

Chapter 5

The Urgency of Now

Having examined mediated misogynoir by exploring media culture, film text, viral videos, television tropes, and documentary, I return to the concept of knowing, and what it means to be an innocent and knowing Black child. As a girl growing up in West Baltimore, the urban legend of the "Bunnyman" was about a naked Black man who wandered through both Leakin and Druid Hill parks, attempting to snatch unsuspecting boys and girls, tie them to a tree, and sodomize them or, in our adolescent shorthand, "bun them." No one I knew had ever actually *seen* the Bunnyman, but everyone *knew* about him and the need to stay alert when in the parks. I was 13 years old and alone in Druid Hill Park, waiting for my best male friend G. and his three male friends to meet me and continue the walk to my house for an afternoon of listening to music. As I listened to Guns-n-Roses on my headphones, I felt a presence near me, looked over my shoulder, and saw the Bunnyman. He was a dark-skinned man, oiled and naked, except for a white knit skullcap, white gloves, and white athletic shoes. His dark brown eyes bore into mine, and he held his index finger up to his lips and mimed, "Shhh." On instinct, I picked up a large rock near my feet and hurled it at him. I then crossed onto a median strip and continued hurling rocks at him. Within seconds, I saw my male friends casually walking toward me, and I screamed, "The Bunnyman tried to grab me!" I pointed to the naked man. The boys gave chase, the Bunnyman retreated back into the woods.

Alone on the median strip, I did not cry. I did feel proud of my quick reflexes. In the fifteen minutes of waiting for my friends to return, I realized I was still alone. No one had stayed behind with me. The boys returned—the Bunnyman had gotten away, but my friends were slapping each other on the back, recounting the thrill of the chase, cracking jokes. They were high off their now validated masculinity. I was silent and began walking home. They followed, still congratulating each other, and laughing. No one asked how I was doing or asked about what I experienced. Just before we reached my block, I turned and told the boys that I did not feel like hanging out anymore. We parted ways.

I realized that boys truly experience the world differently than girls. The experience was liberating for them and limiting for me. They could walk, run, and whoop freely through the woods, but those same woods held a new level of danger for me. I knew that I needed to always wear athletic shoes so I could run to save myself. I also knew I could not tell my mother about this incident, or she would prevent me from roaming the woods—something I loved. Braving the stairs of our row home and stepping into the vestibule, the air felt different. Oppressive. Then I entered the bright, yellow kitchen where my mother sat at the table with her head in her hands. I asked her what was wrong. She told me that a dear relative was just raped, having been dragged into the woods during her morning jog.

I believe that in our bid to quantify the ways Black girls' adultification hinders their quality of life, we often fail to ask, "when is knowing too much a good thing?" What if knowing protects Black girls and keeps them safe in a hostile world, just as much as it sets them up for victimization? Black women's and girls' "knowing" is as much a double bind as DuBoisian double-consciousness. How do we validate the power of Black women's and girls' instinctual self-protection while also viewing them with a gaze broad enough and empathetic enough to hold all their complexity, emotional fluidity, and contradictions?

It is urgently important that we answer these questions. The speed at which the global world is hurtling toward increased migration due to climate change and war and the inevitable transition of neoliberal economics to global corporatocracy impacts Black women's and girls' livelihood on multiple fronts. One in five Black women in the U.S. has experienced rape at some point during their lives (Black et al. 2011, 2). In K-12 schools, Black girls represent 8 percent of enrollment but 13 percent of student suspension (CRDC 2016). Black girls constitute 14 percent of the general population nationally, but 33.2 percent of girls detained and committed to prisons. Black women have higher maternal mortality rates (MMWR 2019), higher diagnoses of mental disorders, and trail behind their White female and male coworkers in terms of wages and employment outcomes (NCBCP 2019). The statistics are daunting. However, Black women are hailed as the most educated group in the U.S (Helm 2016). Black women and girls are dominating in traditionally White sports such as tennis and gymnastics. Black women are making Hollywood films and television shows. Black women like Stacy Abrams are initiating political campaigns in ways reminiscent of foremothers like Shirley Chisolm. The "both/and-ness" of Black women's and girls' lives in the U.S. is a microcosm of the larger ecosystem. In 1977, the Combahee River Collective made the clear argument that Black women are "inherently valuable and our liberation is a necessity not as an adjunct to somebody else but because of our need as human persons for autonomy" (Taylor et al., 2017, 2). As the group in the U.S that holds the burden of this country's inability to eradicate racism, classism, sexism, homophobia, and heterosexism, to liberate Black women and girls is to liberate all others.

COMBATING MEDIATED MISOGYNOIR

In a society of increased media spectacle and surveillance, it is imperative that we merge the work of Black feminist and Black digital humanities scholars, cultural workers, activists, and healers to develop new frameworks to understand Black women's and girls' pain and resistance in all forms of media culture. Black feminist theory (BFT) is a "critical social theory that identifies and deconstructs epistemologies that negate the lived experiences of Black females, and serves . . . as a platform to support the development of critical literacy and more specifically, critical media literacy skills to resist these dominant ways of thinking about Black females' identity" (Robinson, Allen-Handy and Craft 2021, 80) Black feminist media studies (BFMS) are a "growing body of scholarly work that looks at the intersection of media race, and gender, with a specific focus on women of African descent" (Keeling 2008). BFMS is broad enough to combat mediated misogynoir from a myriad of positions. Black feminist media studies explore the ways mediated representations impact the cultural, economic, and political lives of Black women. As a Black media scholar trained in American Studies and employed in a media and film studies department, I find myself pulling from multiple, often disparate sources to understand the complexities of Black women's and girls' mediated lives. Black feminist scholars develop robust critiques and conceptualizations across fields and mediums including Black studies, digital humanities, ethnic studies, history, English, sociology, media studies, and blog posts on a variety of platforms. With a dedicated framework guiding our efforts, Black feminist media scholars can have as much impact on the field of media studies as the Combahee River Collective's articulation of liberation had on feminist studies. I believe it is time that we concentrate our efforts as Black scholars, cultural workers, activists, and healers on creating frameworks that validate Black women's and girls' ways of knowing, and re-visibilize Black women's and girls' humanity. To do so, I believe Black feminist media studies can: 1) illuminate the workings of misogynoir in mediated representations of Black women's and girls' pain; 2) commit to validating Black women's and girls' ways of knowing; and 3) develop techniques to combat empty empathy, especially in viral environments.

For years, much Black media scholarship has been dedicated to debunking representational politics set forth by the White media culture industry. While this work is important, especially as a vehicle for identifying opportunities for repair, I believe scholarly investigations must turn *inward* to garner narrative justice for Black women and girls. With an increase in Black media makers and platforms for Black cultural work, I believe it is imperative that Black feminist media studies explore film, television, broadcast and print news and digital media created by Black media cultural workers. Black feminist media studies must continue the critical analysis of the work of Black female media makers. This scholarship must commit to helping develop accurate, nuanced, and new configurations of mediated representations of Black women and girls that do not solely highlight progress narratives. Black feminist media studies can also develop additional theories of spectatorship that are not solely dedicated to oppositional investigations of texts but also focus on examining the both/and-ness of Black women's and girls' viewing practices. Finally, Black feminist media scholarship can establish and help implement Black feminist media-making practices to guide the creation of robust and nimble representations of Black women's and girls' lives.

An important approach to combating mediated misogynoir is embracing and elevating grounded theory that comes from the most marginalized of us. We must expand the call for solidarity with Black transwomen, non-binary communities, gender non-conforming people, and economically precarious people. As the originator of the theory of misogynoir, Moya Bailey's digital alchemy offers great promise in combating the phenomena. In *Misogynoir Transformed: Black Women's Digital Resistance*, Baily "examines the social media activities of Black women as one way that they are attempting to redress the negative impact of stereotypes in their lives and on their health" (2021, 11). Bailey uses multiple case studies to show how Black women, non-binary, agender, and gender variant people resist misogynoir by creating their own digital content-re-writing problematic representations of themselves. Framing this approach as harm reduction, digital alchemy acknowledges the fact that harm is part and parcel of the world of representation that is anti-Black, anti-women, anti-nonbinary, and anti-gender variant. Digital alchemy can be both a defensive response, a recalibration of misogynoir, and a generative science that creates new types of representation that speak to the specific communities that have been harmed. Bailey's digital alchemy is a welcome approach to media analysis that moves beyond cataloguing artifacts of misogynoir and lamenting negative representations to highlight Black women, non-binary, agender and gender variant people's resistance and agency.

As Black feminists, we must continue developing, archiving, and critically evaluating new modes of activism. In the U.S., Black women are the leaders in digital activism And as such, concerted efforts to understand

Black women's and girls' hashtag activism fits within the scope of BFMS. Hashtags elevate public debates in places where digital access is abundant (Gulla 2014). Hashtag campaigns such as #sayhername, #muterkelly #metoo, #blackgirlmagic all do the important work of shaping and making visible the needs of Black women and girls. Hashtag activism must also find unique ways of bridging the gap between digital and on the ground organizing. In a society of media spectacle and surveillance, hashtag campaigns can promote a false sense of solidarity and movement success. We are not taught activist history in the classroom; we are taught the history of empire and imperialism. Hashtag campaigns run the risk of lulling people into a false sense of accomplishment if not paired with direct action.

Black feminist media studies must engage those who praise, those who twerk, and those who do both. Investigations into mediated representation of rachet feminism, such as Ashley Payne's exploration of the "Cardi-B-Beyonce" (2020) continuum on Black adolescent girls' concepts of respectability in school settings allows an additional avenue to make legible Black girls' responses to violent disciplinary policies in education. In her ethnographic research, Payne found, "the girls within this Black girlhood celebratory space continually worked within the nexus of Hip Hop and Blackness girlhood, challenging, critiquing, and (re)constructing notions of Black girlhood, particularly as it relates to ratchet-Black girlhood. They expressed a need for spaces where they can be themselves and transformed their educational space into a space that was just that: a place for them to be who they want to be, free from the gaze of others" (Payne 2020, 16). This observation shows how rachet feminism scholarship offers recuperative approaches to mediated misogynoir. We may balk at Beyonce's version of capitalist feminist activism, but we also must investigate her shine to examine which parts of her argument may be liberatory.

We must also see threads of solidarity among victim-survivors of gender-based violence and intimate partner violence. Julia Jordan-Zachery's investigation into the way Black magazine platforms, Black political representatives and Black blogs have all used universalizing language to obscure the specific ways intimate partner violence manifests in Black women's lives is one prime example of this scholarship (2017). Another important thread of scholarship capable of combating mediated misogynoir focuses on contemporary and historical trauma, as well as people's responses to this trauma in a mediated environment. Patrice Douglass's *Black Feminist Theory for the Dead and Dying* is an examination of the rhetoric used in 2017 Women's March's in relation to the 2016 murder of Korryn Gaines by the Baltimore Special Weapons and Tactics (SWAT) team. She illustrates "how the specificities of Blackness are crowded out by the drive towards a collective politic" (2018, 1). Douglass works hard to reconcile the fact that Black feminist theory has a difficult time holding Afro-pessimism as just Afro-pessimism, often writes gender "into the void" even though it benefits from Hortense Spiller's Black feminism. Both Black Feminism and Afro-Pessimism are promising fields for exploration of the both/and-ness of Black women's and girls' humanity. Resmanaa Menakem's 2017 My *Grandmother's Hands: Racialized Trauma and the Pathway to Mending Our Hearts and Bodies*, though not a text about media, offers a way to explore how mediated narratives of Black women's and girls' trauma can live in our bodies. An awareness of the images that trigger harm can help combat the creation of misogynoir-laden texts about Black women and girls.

Another helpful theory to combat mediated misogynoir is Joy James' theory of the captive maternal—biological females or those feminized into caretaking and consumption. Captive maternals are most "vulnerable to violence, war, poverty, police, and captivity; those whose very existence enables the possessive empire that claims and dispossesses them" (2018, 250). Captive maternals can range from Stacy Abrams helping mobilize disenfranchised voters in Georgia to local activists who organize candlelit vigils after state violence. The liberation work of captive maternals is often celebrated in mediated environments but is rarely made structural. As James laments, "we keep our communities functioning. We will not abandon them because we love them. But, every time we stabilize our communities, the state builds upon that stability to stabilize itself. So, what's next for the captive maternal? What's the exit plan?" (257). The concept of captive maternals provides an evocative framework for understanding how online activism both liberates and fails Black women and girls.

Combating mediated misogynoir also means developing frameworks for critical media literacy. An increase in critical media literacy helps people identify representative distortions developed by those outside and within the Black community. It is also a key tool in the development of a "framework for positive Black female identity formation" (Robinson, Allan-Handy, Craft 2021, 86). I am a scholar and a filmmaker. My academic and creative research explores the impact of race and gender-based trauma on Black identity development and Black cultural production. As a filmmaker, I specifically interrogate ways to combat the numbing effect of watching viral videos of Black pain, wounding, and death through embodied image schema analysis (Young, Kim 2021). This work actively combats the spectacular and surveillance culture that allows mediated misogynoir to travel and regard victims and survivors of state-violence as memes instead of full humans who deserve justice. The approaches that have been discussed offer opportunities to develop and strengthen the grounded, reflexive, and nimble theories of the self and the revolution that emerges from Black feminist thought.

We must expand theories about mediated depictions of Black women and girls outside of the legacy of imperial fantasy. While the ghosts of Mammy, Jezebel, Sapphire, and Matriarch might haunt our ways of reading Black women and girls, we also must make room for Baby Mamas, Black Girl Nerds, Futurist Hybrids, Fat Goddesses, and the Orishas among us. Newer conceptions of Black women and girls are flooding our mediated landscape, impacting our real physical lives—containers that facilitate the fluidity of Black women and girls, our both/and-ness and wholly futurist existences are sorely needed.

Bibliography

"*About Sexual Assault*." National Sexual Violence Resource Center. Accessed October 24, 2020. https://www.nsvrc.org/about–sexual–assault.

Allcott, Hunt, and Matthew Gentzkow. 2017. "Social Media and Fake News in the 2016 Election." *Journal of Economic Perspectives* 31, no. 2 (May): 211–36. https://doi.org/10.1257/jep.31.2.211.

"Annenberg Inclusion Initiative." USC Annenberg School for Communication and Journalism. Accessed October 30, 2020. https://annenberg.usc.edu/research/aii.

Ataiyero, Stacy St Clair and Kayce T. 2008. "Why the Jury Acquitted R. Kelly." *Chicago Tribune*. June 14, 2008. https://www.chicagotribune.com/news/ct–xpm–2008–06–14–0806140185–story.html.

Austin, William G., and Stephen Worchel, eds 1979. *The Social Psychology of Intergroup Relations*. Monterey: Brooks/Cole Pub. C.

Bailey, Moya. 2016. "Misogynoir in Medical Media: On Caster Semenya and R. Kelly." *Catalyst: Feminism, Theory, Technoscience* 2, no. 2 (September): 1–31. https://doi.org/10.28968/cftt.v2i2.28800.

———.2021. *Misogynoir Transformed: Black Women's Digital Resistance*. Intersections : Transdisciplinary Perspectives on Genders and Sexualities. New York: New York University Press.

———. 2018. "On Misogynoir: Citation, Erasure, and Plagiarism." *Feminist Media Studies* 18, no. 4 (July): 762–68. https://doi.org/10.1080/14680777.2018.1447395.

Baker, Courtney. 2020. " Operation Catsuit ." *ASAP Journal*, 101, no.2. (July). http://asapjournal.com/b–o–s–10–2–operation–catsuit–courtney–r–baker/.

Ball, James. 2020. *The Tangled Web We Weave: Inside the Shadow System That Shapes the Internet*. Brooklyn: Melville House.

Barboza, Craigh. 2016. "Boyz n the Hood at 25: A Look Back at 1991's Black Film Renaissance." *Washington Post*, July 2, 2016. https://www.washingtonpost.com/lifestyle/boyz–n–the–hood–at–25–a–look–back–at–1991s–black–film–renaissance/2016/06/30/6c0bb6c4–3c9d–11e6–84e8–1580c7db5275_story.html.

Barnes, Dee. 2015. "Here's What's Missing From *Straight Outta Compton*: Me and the Other Women Dr. Dre Beat Up." *Gawker*. August 18, 2015. https://www.gawker.com/heres–whats–missing–from–straight–outta–compton–me–and–1724735910

Bent–Goodley, T. B. 2009. "A Black Experience–Based Approach to Gender–Based Violence." *Social Work* 54, no. 3 (July): 262–69. https://doi.org/10.1093/sw/54.3.262.

Berg, Madeline. "How 'Empire' Became The Most Valuable Show On Broadcast TV." *Forbes*. May 20, 2017. https://www.forbes.com/sites/maddieberg/2017/03/20/how–empire–became–the–most–valuable–show–on–broadcast–tv/.

Black, MC, and KC Basil. "The National Intimate Partner and Sexual Violence Survey (NISVS): 2010 Summary Report." CDC, 2011. https://www.cdc.gov/violenceprevention/pdf/NISVS_Report2010–a.pdf.

Bloodsworth–Lugo, Mary K, and Dan Flory. 2013. *Race, Philosophy, and Film.* Hoboken: Taylor and Francis.

Bobo, Jacqueline. 1998. "Black Women's Responses to 'The Color Purple." no. 33 (Feb): 43–51. https://www.ejumpcut.org/archive/onlinessays/JC33folder/ClPurpleBobo.html.

Bogle, Donald. 2016. *Toms, Coons, Mulattoes, Mammies, and Bucks: An Interpretive History of Blacks in American Films.* 5th ed. New York: Continuum.

Bordalejo, Barbara, and Roopika Risam, eds. 2019. *Intersectionality in Digital Humanities.* (Collection Development, Cultural Heritage, and Digital Humanities). Leeds: Arc Humanities Press.

Bowser, Pearl, and Louise Spence. "Oscar Micheaux's 'Body and Soul' and the Burden of Representation." *Cinema Journal* 39, no. 3 (2000): 3–29. https://www.jstor.org/stable/1225531.

Boylorn, Robin. "From Boys to Men: Hip–Hop, Hood Films, and the Performance of Contemporary Black Masculinity." *Black Camera* 8, no. 2 (2017): 146. https://doi.org/10.2979/blackcamera.8.2.09.

Brade, Kesslyn A, and Tricia Bent–Goodly. 2009. "A Refuge for My Soul: Examining African American Clergy's Perceptions Related to Domestic Violence Awareness and Engagement in Faith Community Initiatives." *Social Work and Christianity* 36, no. 4 (Winter): 430–48.

Broussard, Patricia A. 2013. "Black Women's Post–Slavery Silence Syndrome: A Twenty–First Century Remnant of Slavery, Jim Crow, and Systemic Racism – Who Will Tell Her Stories?" *The Journal of Gender, Race & Justice* 16 (April): 373. https://search.ebscohost.com/login.aspx?direct=true&db=edslex&AN=edslex45E6 7D6E&site=eds–live&scope=site.

Browne, Simone. 2015. *Dark Matters: On the Surveillance of Blackness.* Durham: Duke University Press.

Bumiller, Kristin. 2008. *In an Abusive State: How Neoliberalism Appropriated the Feminist Movement against Sexual Violence.* Durham: Duke University Press.

Butchart, Alexander, Claudia Garcia–Moreno, Christopher Mikton, World Health Organization, and London School of Hygiene and Tropical Medicine. 2010. *Preventing Intimate Partner and Sexual Violence against Women: Global Trends and Determinants of Prevalence, Safety, and Acceptability.* Geneva: World Health Organization. http://whqlibdoc.who.int/publications/2010/9789241564007_eng.pdf.

Butler, Judith. 1993. "Endangered/Endangering: Schematic Racism and White Paranoia." In *Reading Rodney King/Reading Urban Uprising*, edited by Robert Gooding–Williams, 15–22. New York: Routledge.

Butler, Paul. 2013. "Black Male Exceptionalism? The Problems and Potential of Black Male–Focused Interventions." *DuBois Review: Social Science Research on Race* 10, no. 2 (2013): 485–511. https://doi.org/10.1017/S1742058X13000222.

Cadet, Danielle. 2014. "The 'Straight Outta Compton' Casting Call Is So Offensive It Will Make Your Jaw Drop." *HuffPost,* July 17, 2014. https://www.huffpost.com/entry/straight–out–of–compton–casting–call_n_5597010.

Callahan, Yesha. 2015. "Lee Daniels Responds to Tavis Smiley's Critique of Empire." *The Grapevine.* April 9, 2015. https://thegrapevine.theroot.com/lee–daniels–responds–to–tavis–smiley–s–critique–of–empi–1790886393.

Carbado, Devon W. 2005. "Privilege." In *Black Queer Studies*, edited by E. Patrick Johnson and Mae G. Henderson, 190–212. Durham: Duke University Press. https://doi.org/10.1215/9780822387220–011.

Carey, Tamika L. 2018. "A Tightrope of Perfection: The Rhetoric and Risk of Black Women's Intellectualism on Display in Television and Social Media." *Rhetoric Society Quarterly* 48, no. 2 (March): 139–60. https://doi.org/10.1080/02773945.2017.1392037.

Chetty, Raj, Nathaniel Hendren, Maggie Jones, and Sonya Porter. "Race and Economic Opportunity in the United States: An Intergenerational Perspective." NEBR Working Paper 2441 National Bureau of Economic Research Cambridge, MA, March 2018. https://doi.org/10.3386/w24441.

Chow, Andrew, and Joshua Bates. 2019. "A Full Timeline of Sexual Abuse Allegations Against R. Kelly." *Time.* August 6, 2019. https://time.com/5546990/r–kelly–timeline/.

Coard, Stephanie Irby, Alfiee M. Breland, and Patricia Raskin. 2006. "Perceptions of and Preferences for Skin Color, Black Racial Identity, and Self–Esteem among African Americans." *Journal of Applied Social Psychology* 31, no. 11 (July): 2256–2274. https://doi.org/10.1111/j.1559–1816.2001.tb00174.x.

Collins, Patricia Hill. 2009. *Black Feminist Thought: Knowledge, Consciousness, and the Politics of Empowerment*. 2nd ed. Routledge Classics. New York: Routledge, 2009.

———. 2004. *Black Sexual Politics: African Americans, Gender, and the New Racism*. New York: Routledge.

Cooper, Brittney C., Susana M. Morris, and Robin M. Boylorn, eds. 2017. *The Crunk Feminist Collection*. New York: The Feminist Press at CUNY. Kindle.

Craig, Maxine Leeds. 2002. *Ain't I a Beauty Queen? Black Women, Beauty, and the Politics of Race*. United Kingdom: Oxford University Press.

Creed, Barbara. 1993. *The Monstrous–Feminine: Film, Feminism, Psychoanalysis*. New York: Routledge.

Crenshaw, Kimberlé. 2006. "Framing Affirmative Action." *Michigan Law Review First Impressions* 105, no. 1 (January): 123–33. https://repository.law.umich.edu/mlr_fi/vol105/iss1/4.

Crenshaw, Kimberlé, and Andrea Ritchie. 2015. "Say Her Name: Resisting Police Brutality Against Black Women." *African American Policy Forum*. https://aapf. org/shnreport.

"Cultural News Roundup: Black Girls Matter, Caitlyn Jenner & Representations Of Trans Women, Police Response To McKinney, Texas Pool Party & More." *The Marc Steiner Show*. https://www.steinershow.org/podcasts/cultural–news–roundup–black–girls–matter–caitlyn–jenner–representations–of–trans–women–police–response–to–mckinney–texas–pool–party–more/.

Daer, Alice R., Rebecca Hoffman, and Seth Goodman. 2014. "Rhetorical Functions of Hashtag Forms Across Social Media Applications." In *Proceedings of the 32nd ACM International Conference on The Design of Communication CD–ROM – SIGDOC '14*, 1–3. Colorado Springs: ACM Press, https://doi.org/10.1145/2666216.2666231.

Daniels, Jessie. 2013. "Race and Racism in Internet Studies: A Review and Critique." *New Media & Society* 15, no. 5 (August): 695–719. https://doi. org/10.1177/1461444812462849.

D'Argembeau, Arnaud, Claudia Lardi, and Martial Van der Linden. 2012. "Self–Defining Future Projections: Exploring the Identity Function of Thinking about the Future." *Memory* 20, no. 2 (February): 110–20. https://doi.org/10.1080/09658 211.2011.647697.

Davis, Angela Y. 1981. "Rape, Racism and the Capitalist Setting." *The Black Scholar* 12, no. 6 (November): 39–45. https://doi.org/10.1080/00064246.1981.11414219.

Davis, Bradford William. 2020. "Like Many Black Women in Media, Gayle King Was Attacked for Doing Her Job." *nydailynews.com*. February 8, 2020. https://www. nydailynews.com/sports/ny–gayle–king–kobe–bryant–lisa–leslie–20200208–znarqjfz4rfd3pdwh765gxbdzq–story.html.

Debord, Guy. 2004. *The Society of the Spectacle*. New York: Zone Books.

DeFrantz, Thomas, and Anita Gonzalez, eds. 2014. *Black Performance Theory*. Durham: Duke University Press.

Diawara, Manthia, ed. 1993. *Black American Cinema*. AFI Film Readers. New York: Routledge.

Dicker/Sun, Glenda. 2005. "Katrina: Acting Black / Playing Blackness." *Theatre Journal* 57, no. 4 (December): 614–16. https://www.jstor.org/stable/25069732.

Donalson, Melvin Burke. 2003. *Black Directors in Hollywood*. Austin: University of Texas Press.

Dougherty, Cristy, and Bernadette Marie Calafell. 2019. "Before and Beyond #MeToo and #TimesUp: Rape as a Colonial and Racist Project." *Women & Language* 42 (1): 181–85. doi:10.34036/WL.2019.021.

Doughty, Ruth. 2016. "The Buppie and Authentic Blackness." *Film International* 14, no. 3 (December): 125–40. https://doi.org/10.1386/fiin.14.3–4.125_1.

Douglass, Patrice D. 2018. "Black Feminist Theory for the Dead and Dying." *Theory & Event* 21, no. 1 (January): 106–23. https://muse.jhu.edu/article/685972.

Eazy E.1988. *Eazy–Duz–It*. Ruthless/Priority Records 4XL57100, cassette.

Ellis, Aimé J, and Aim J Ellis. 2014. *If We Must Die From Bigger Thomas to Biggie Smalls*. Detroit: Wayne University Press.

Ellison, Sarah, and Bethonie Butler. 2020. "Gayle King's Response to Kobe Bryant Backlash Captures the Unique Pressures She Faces as One of the Most Visible Black Women in Media." *The Washington Post*, February 7, 2020.

Ellithorpe, Morgan E., and Amy Bleakley. 2016. "Wanting to See People Like Me? Racial and Gender Diversity in Popular Adolescent Television." *Journal of Youth and Adolescence* 45, no. 7 (July): 1426–37. https://doi.org/10.1007/s10964–016–0415–4.

Ellithorpe, Morgan E., Michael Hennessy, and Amy Bleakley. 2019."Adolescent Perceptions of Black–Oriented Media: 'The Day Beyoncé Turned Black': Can Black–Oriented Films and TV Programs Be Marketed More Broadly?" *Journal of Advertising Research* 59, no. 2 (June): 158–70. https://doi.org/10.2501/JAR–2018–017.

Empire. Drama, Music. Lee Daniels Entertainment, Danny Strong Productions, Little Chicken Productions, 2015.

Epstein, Rebecca, Jamilia Blake, and Thalia Gonzzlez. 2017. "Girlhood Interrupted: The Erasure of Black Girls Childhood." *SSRN Electronic Journal*. https://doi.org/10.2139/ssrn.3000695.

Erigha, Maryann. 2015. "Shonda Rhimes, Scandal, and the Politics of Crossing Over." *The Black Scholar* 45, no. 1 (January): 10–15. https://doi.org/10.1080/00064246.2014.997598.

———. 2019. *The Hollywood Jim Crow: The Racial Politics of the Movie Industry*. New York: New York University Press.

Everett, Anna. 2009. *Digital Diaspora: A Race for Cyberspace*. Albany: SUNY Press.

Faughnder, Ryan, and Stacy Perman. 2020."Black Filmmakers and Executives Get Honest about Their Experiences in Hollywood." *Press Herald*, June 17, 2020. https://www.pressherald.com/2020/06/17/black–filmmakers–and–executives–get–honest–about–their–experiences–in–hollywood.

Finoh, Maya and Sankofa, Jasmine. 2019. "The Legal System Has Failed Black Girls, Women, and Non–Binary Survivors of Violence." *aclu.org*. January 28, 2019. https://www.aclu.org/blog/racial–justice/race–and–criminal–justice/legal–system–has–failed–black–girls–women–and–non.

Firth, Raymond. 2011. *Symbols: Public and Private*. London: Routledge.

Fisher, Celeste A. *Black on Black: Urban Youth Films and the Multicultural Audience*. Lanham, Md: Scarecrow Press, 2006.

Fleetwood, Nicole R. 2015. *On Racial Icons: Blackness and the Public Imagination*. New Brunswick: Rutgers University Press.

———. 2011. *Troubling Vision: Performance, Visuality, and Blackness*. Chicago: The University of Chicago Press.

Fortner, Robert S. 1991. "Remote Control: Television, Audiences, and Cultural Power." *American Journalism* (8): 201–203. httip://doi.org/10.1080/08821127.1991.10731361.

Foster, John Bellamy, and Robert W. McChesney. 2014."Surveillance Capitalism: Monopoly–Finance Capital, the Military–Industrial Complex, and the Digital Age." *Monthly Review* 66, no. 3 (July): 1–31. https://doi.org/10.14452/MR–066–03–2014–07_1.

Gallon, Kim. 2016. "Making a Case for the Black Digital Humanities." In *Debates in the Digital Humanities 2016*, edited by Matthew K. Gold and Lauren F. Klein, 42–49. Minneapolis: University of Minnesota Press. https://doi.org/10.5749/j.ctt1cn6thb.7.

Garcia, Sandra E. 2017. "The Woman Who Created #MeToo Long Before Hashtags." *The New York Times*, October 20, 2017. https://www.nytimes.com/2017/10/20/us/me–too–movement–tarana–burke.html.

Gilliam, Dorothy Butler. 2018. "It's Time to Recognize the Role of the Black Press in the Civil Rights Movement." *NBC News*. March 24, 2018. https://www.nbcnews.com/think/opinion/critical–role–black–press–civil–rights–movement–has–not–received–ncna859701.

Gilliam, Franklin D., Nicholas A. Valentino, and Matthew N. Beckmann. 2002. "Where You Live and What You Watch: The Impact of Racial Proximity and Local Television News on Attitudes about Race and Crime." *Political Research Quarterly* 55, no. 4 (December): 755–80. https://doi.org/10.1177/106591290205500402.

Gilman, Sander L. 1985. "Black Bodies, White Bodies: Toward an Iconography of Female Sexuality in Late Nineteenth–Century Art, Medicine, and Literature." *Critical Inquiry* 12, no. 1 (Autumn): 204–42. https://www.jstor.org/stable/1343468.

Gilmore, Leigh. 2017. *Tainted Witness: Why We Doubt What Women Say about Their Lives*. New York: Columbia University Press.

Gilmore, Ruth Wilson. 1993. "Terror Austerity: Race Gender Excess Theater." In *Reading Rodney King/Reading Urban Uprising*, edited by Robert Gooding–Williams, 23–35. New York: Routledge.

Gilroy, Paul. 1993. *The Black Atlantic: Modernity and Double Consciousness*. Cambridge: Harvard University Press.

Goldman, Adria Y., ed. 2014. *Black Women and Popular Culture: The Conversation Continues*. Lanham: Lexington Books.

Gonick, Marnina. 2010. "Indigenizing Girl Power: The *Whale Rider.* Decolonization, and the Project of Remembering." *Feminist Media Studies* 10, no. 3 (September): 305–19. https://doi.org/10.1080/14680777.2010.493648.

Grady, Constance. "The Complicated, Inadequate Language of Sexual Violence." Vox, November 30, 2017. https://www.vox.com/culture/2017/11/30/16644394/language–sexual–violence.

Gray, F. Gary, Director. 2016. *Straight Outta Compton*. Universal Studios Home Entertainment. https://search.ebscohost.com/login.aspx?direct=true&db=cat01451a&AN=towson.004673472&site=eds–live&scope=site.

Greene, Beverly. 2000. "African American Lesbian and Bisexual Women." *Journal of Social Issues* 56, no. 2 (January): 239–49. https://doi.org/10.1111/0022–4537.00163.

Guadagno, Rosanna & Rempala, Daniel & Murphy, Shannon & Okdie, Bradley. 2013. "Why do Internet Videos Go Viral? A Social Influence Analysis." Computers in Human Behavior.

Guthrie, Marisa. 2019. "The Anchor: Gayle King and CBS News' Plans to Steady a Once–Storied Ship." *Hollywood Reporter*." June 12, 2019, https://www.hollywoodreporter.com/features/gayle–king–cbs–news–woes–charlie–rose–r–kelly–staying–at–cbs–1217434.

Haag, Matthew. 2018. "Black Woman's Violent Arrest at Alabama Waffle House Was Justified, Police Say." *The New York Times,* April 24, 2019. https://search. ebscohost.com/login.aspx?direct=true&db=edsnex&AN=edsnex.5S5X.59K1. JBG3.625T.00000.00&site=eds–live&scope=site.

Hall, Ronald E. 2018. "The Bleaching Syndrome per Colorism Pathology: Lgbtq Perpetuation of Discrimination." *American Behavioral Scientist* 62, no. 14 (December): 2055–71. https://doi.org/10.1177/0002764218810759.

Hall, Stefan and Pasquini, Silvia. 2020. "Can There Be a Happy Ending for Hollywood after COVID–19?" *World Economic Forum.* July 23, 2020. https://www.weforum.org/agenda/2020/07/ impact–coronavirus–covid–19–hollywood–global–film–industry–movie–theatres/.

Hall, Stuart, David Morley, and Kuan–Hsing Chen, eds.1996. *Stuart Hall: Critical Dialogues in Cultural Studies.* New York: Routledge.

Hallas, Roger. 2007. "Sound, Image and Corporeal Implication of Witnessing in Derek Jarmin's Blue." In *The Image and the Witness,* edited by Frances Guerin. London: Wallflower Press.

Hamilton, Anthony, vocalist. 2006. "Sista Big Bones." NP3 audio. Track 9 on *Ain't Nobody Worryin,* So So Def.

Hampton, Dream, Director. 2019. *Surviving R. Kelly.* Aired January 3, 2019, on Lifetime.

Hanna, Monica, Jennifer Harford Vargas, and José David Saldívar. 2016. eds. *Junot Díaz and the Decolonial Imagination.* Durham: Duke University Press.

Haney–López, Ian. 2014. *Dog Whistle Politics: How Coded Racial Appeals Have Reinvented Racism and Wrecked the Middle Class.* New York: Oxford University Press.

Harris–Perry, Melissa V. 2011. *Sister Citizen: Shame, Stereotypes, and Black Women in America.* New Haven: Yale University Press.

Harkins, Gillian. 2009. *Everybody's Family Romance: Reading Incest in Neoliberal America.* Minneapolis: University of Minnesota Press.

Hartman, Saidiya V. 1997. *Scenes of Subjection: Terror, Slavery, and Self–Making in Nineteenth–Century America.* New York: Oxford University Press.

Hauser, Christine. 2020. "Snoop Dogg Apologizes After Criticizing Gayle King Over Kobe Bryant Questions." *The New York Times,* February 13, 2020. https://www. nytimes.com/2020/02/13/business/media/snoop–dogg–apologizes–gayle–king. html.

Haynes, Chayla, Saran Stewart, and Evette Allen. 2016. "Three Paths, One Struggle: Black Women and Girls Battling Invisibility in U.S. Classrooms." *The Journal of Negro Education* 85, no. 3 (Summer): 380–91. https://doi.org/10.7709/ jnegroeducation.85.3.0380.

Helm, Angela Bronner. 2016. "Black Women Now the Most Educated Group in US." *The Root.* June 5, 2016. https://www.theroot.com/ black–women–now–the–most–educated–group–in–us–1790855540.

Herman, Judith Lewis. *Trauma and Recovery.* 2015 edition. New York: Basic Books.

Hester, Helen, and Caroline Walters. 2016. "Introduction: Theorizing Fat Sex." *Sexualities* 19, no. 8 (December): 893–97. https://doi.org/10.1177/1363460716640728.

Hill, Mark E. 2002. "Skin Color and the Perception of Attractiveness among African Americans: Does Gender Make a Difference?" *Social Psychology Quarterly* 65, no. 1 (March): 77. https://doi.org/10.2307/3090169.

Hill, Nicole. 2016. "Intimate Partner Abuse Among African American Same Gender–Involved Females: A Collision at the Intersection of Poverty, Trauma, Mental Health Symptoms, and Racialized, Sexist, Heterocentrism." PhD diss., Howard University.

Hobson, Janell. 2015. "Straight Outta Compton and the Power of Black Women's "Side Stories."" *Ms. Magazine*. August 24, 2015. https://msmagazine.com/2015/08/24/straight–outta–compton–and–the–power–of–black–womens–side–stories/.

Hogan, Bernie. 2010. "The Presentation of Self in the Age of Social Media: Distinguishing Performances and Exhibitions Online." *Bulletin of Science, Technology & Society* 30, no. 6 (December): 377–86. https://doi.org/10.1177/0270467610385893.

Holloway, Karla FC. 2002. *Passed On: African American Mourning Stories, A Memorial*. Durham: Duke University Press. https://doi.org/10.1215/9780822385073.

Holmes, Rachel. 2020. *The Hottentot Venus: The Life and Death of Saartjie Baartman: Born 1789 – Buried 2002*. London: Bloomsbury Press.

hooks, bell. 2015. *Black Looks: Race and Representation*. New York: Routledge, 2015.

———. 1997. Cultural Criticism and Transformation. Television, 1997. https://www.mediaed.org/transcripts/Bell–Hooks–Transcript.pdf.

Hughey, Matthew W. 2009. "Cinethetic Racism: White Redemption and Black Stereotypes in 'Magical Negro' Films." *Social Problems* 56, no. 3 (August): 543–77. https://doi.org/10.1525/sp.2009.56.3.543.

Hull, Gloria T., Patricia Bell–Scott, and Barbara Smith, eds. 1982. *All the Women Are White, All the Blacks Are Men, but Some of Us Are Brave: Black Women's Studies*. New York: Feminist Press.

Hunt, Stacy Wilson. 2014. "Lee Daniels on Fox's 'Empire': 'I Wanted to Make a Black "Dynasty"' (Q&A) *Hollywood Reporter*." May 6, 2014. https://www.hollywoodreporter.com/live–feed/lee–daniels–foxs–empire–i–701855.

Impelli, Matthew. 2020. "Snoop Dogg Criticizes Gayle King for Mentioning Kobe Bryant's Sexual Assault Charge in Interview: 'What Do You Gain from That?'" *Newsweek*. February 6, 2020. https://www.newsweek.com/snoop–dogg–criticizes–gayle–king–mentioning–kobe–bryants–sexual–assault–charge–interview–what–1486086.

Jackson, Cassandra. 2011. *Violence, Visual Culture, and the Black Male Body*. New York: Routledge.

Jackson, Sarah J. 2016. "(Re)Imagining Intersectional Democracy from Black Feminism to Hashtag Activism." *Women's Studies in Communication* 39, no. 4 (October): 375–79. https://doi.org/10.1080/07491409.2016.1226654.

Jackson, Sarah J., and Sonia Banaszczyk. 2016. "Digital Standpoints: Debating Gendered Violence and Racial Exclusions in the Feminist Counterpublic." *Journal of Communication Inquiry* 40, no. 4 (October): 391–407. https://doi.org/10.1177/0196859916667731.

Jacobo, Julia. 2016. "Maryland Teen Who Was Pepper–Sprayed by Police Shares Her Side of the Story." *ABC News*. September 23, 2016. https://abcnews.go.com/US/maryland–teen–pepper–sprayed–police–shares–side–story/story?id=42293931.

James, Allison, Chris Jenks, and Alan Prout. 2014. *Theorizing Childhood*. Cambridge: Polity Press.

James, Joy. 2016. "The Womb of Western Theory: Trauma, Time Theft, and the Captive Maternal." *Carceral Notebooks Challenging the Punitive Society,* 12 (November). http://www.thecarceral.org/journal–vol12.html.

Johnson, E. Patrick. 2003. *Appropriating Blackness: Performance and the Politics of Authenticity*. Durham: Duke University Press.

Jones–Deeweaver, Avis. 2019. "The State of Black Women in the U.S. and Key States 2019." Roundtable Summary, n.d.

Jordan–Zachery, Julia S. 2017. *Shadow Bodies: Black Women, Ideology, Representation, and Politics*. New York: Rutgers University Press. https://www.degruyter.com/isbn/9780813593432.

Khan, Matte. 2020. "8 Journalists on Reporting While Black, With the Weight of History on Their Shoulders." *Glamour*. June 3, 2020. https://www.glamour.com/story/8–black–women–journalists–on–reporting–police–brutality.

Kang, Cecilia. 2015. "With Shows like 'Empire,' 'Black–Ish' and 'Cristela,' TV Is More Diverse than Ever." *Washington Post*, January 29, 2015, sec. Business. https://www.washingtonpost.com/business/economy/with–shows–like–empire–black–ish–and–cristela–tv–is–more–diverse–than–ever/2015/01/29/0ac38f82–a576–11e4–a2b2–776095f393b2_story.html.

Keeling, Kara. 2008. "Black Feminist Media Studies." In *The International Encyclopedia of Communication*, edited by Wolfgang Donsbach. Chichester: John Wiley & Sons, Ltd. https://doi.org/10.1002/9781405186407.wbiecb015.

Keith, Verna. 2009. "A Colorstruck World Skin Tone, Achievement, and Self–Esteem Among African American Women." In *Shades of Difference* edited by Evelyn Nakano Glenn. Stanford: Stanford University Press.

Kellner, Douglas. 2020. *Media Culture: Cultural Studies, Identity, and Politics in the Contemporary Moment*. London: Routledge. https://www.taylorfrancis.com/books/9780429244230.

Kelly, Mary Louise. 2020. "Why Memes Around Breonna Taylor's Death Are Not Doing Her Story Any Justice." *NPR.org*. July 10, 2020. https://www.npr.org/2020/07/10/889842746/why–memes–around–breonna–taylors–death–are–not–doing–her–story–any–justice.

Kenny, Maureen C, and Adriana G McEachern. 2000. "Racial, Ethnic, and Cultural Factors of Childhood Sexual Abuse." *Clinical Psychology Review* 20, no. 7 (October): 905–22. https://doi.org/10.1016/S0272–7358(99)00022–7.

Key Data Highlights on Equity and Opportunity Gaps in Our Nation's Public Schools. 2013–2014 Civil Rights Data Collection. A First Look. Revised. 2016. Office for Civil Rights, US Department of Education. https://eric.ed.gov/?id=ED577234.

Kiki. 2018. "An Ode to Fast Ass Girls." *Medium*. July 24, 2018. https://cleoj.medium.com/an–ode–to–the–fast–ass–girls–dda4f1611600.

Kraus, Michael W., Julian M. Rucker, and Jennifer A. Richeson. 2017. "Americans Misperceive Racial Economic Equality." *Proceedings of the National Academy of Sciences of the United States of America* 114, no. 39 (September): 10324–31. https://www.jstor.org/stable/26488023.

Landor, Antoinette M., Leslie Gordon Simons, Ronald L. Simons, Gene H. Brody, Chalandra M. Bryant, Frederick X. Gibbons, Ellen M. Granberg, and Janet N. Melby. 2013. "Exploring the Impact of Skin Tone on Family Dynamics and Race–Related Outcomes." *Journal of Family Psychology* 27, no. 5 (October): 817–26. https://doi.org/10.1037/a0033883.

Lauricella, Alexis R., Ellen Wartella, and Victoria J. Rideout. 2015. "Young Children's Screen Time: The Complex Role of Parent and Child Factors." *Journal of Applied Developmental Psychology* 36 (January): 11–17. https://doi.org/10.1016/j.appdev.2014.12.001.

Lawrance, Benjamin N., and Richard L. Roberts. 2019. "Viral Video 'Blood Chocolate' Activism, Millennial Anti–Trafficking, and the Neoliberal Resurgence of Shaming." *Slavery & Abolition* 40, no. 1 (January): 168–98. https://doi.org/10.1080/0144039X.2018.1475272.

Leach, Colin Wayne, and Aerielle M. Allen. 2017. "The Social Psychology of the Black Lives Matter Meme and Movement." *Current Directions in Psychological Science* 26, no. 6 (December): 543–47. https://doi.org/10.1177/0963721417719319.

Lebduska, Lisa. 2014. "Racist Visual Rhetoric and Images of Trayvon Martin." *Present Tense – A Journal of Rhetoric in Society* 3, no. 2 (April): 1–9. http://www.presenttensejournal.org/.

Lee, Allison H. 2020. "Diversity Matters, Disclosure Works, and the SEC Can Do More: Remarks at the Council of Institutional Investors Fall 2020 Conference." *SEC.Gov.* September 20, 2020. https://www.sec.gov/news/speech/lee–cii–2020–conference–20200922.

Leonard, David J. 2006. *Screens Fade to Black: Contemporary African American Cinema.* Westport, Conn: Praeger Publishers.

Lewis, Reina. 2016."'At the Site of Intimacy': An Interview with Campbell X." *Fashion, Style & Popular Culture* 3, no. 2 (March): 193–207. https://doi.org/10.1386/fspc.3.2.193_1.

Lights Film School. "When Is a Film a Success?" January 18, 2018. https://www.lightsfilmschool.com/blog/when–is–a–film–a–success–afe.

Lockett, Dee. 2015."'Straight Outta Compton' Director Says Dr. Dre's Violence against Women Didn't Fit the Film's Narrative." August 17, 2015. *Business Insider.* https://www.businessinsider.com/dr–dres–violence–against–women–didnt–fit–for–straight–outta–compton–2015–8.

Lundquist, J. H., and K.–H. Lin. 2015. "Is Love (Color) Blind? The Economy of Race among Gay and Straight Daters." *Social Forces* 93, no. 4 (June): 1423–49. https://doi.org/10.1093/sf/sov008.

Lyon, David. *Surveillance, Power, and Everyday Life.* Oxford University Press, 2009. https://doi.org/10.1093/oxfordhb/9780199548798.003.0019.

Madison, D. Soyini. 2010.*Acts of Activism: Human Rights as Radical Performance*. Theatre and Performance Theory. Cambridge: New York, N.Y: Cambridge University Press. Kindle.

Mansell, Robin. 2012. *Imagining the Internet: Communication, Innovation, and Governance*. Oxford: Oxford University Press.

Martin, L. L., Varner, K. J. 2017. "Race, Residential Segregation, and the Death of Democracy: Education and Myth of Postracialism". *Democracy and Education*, 25, no.1, (nd): 1–10 https://doi.org/:10.4324/9781315408705.

Martinelli, Laura Bradley, Marissa. 2015. "Who Are the Women of Straight Outta Compton? Here's What the NWA Biopic Leaves Out." *Slate Magazine*, August 19, 2015. https://slate.com/culture/2015/08/straight–outta–compton–women–the–background–the–nwa–biopic–doesnt–provide–plus–the–women–it–leaves–out.html.

Masullo Chen, Gina, Deepa Fadnis, and Kelsey Whipple. 2020. "Can We Talk About Race? Exploring Online Comments about Race–Related Shootings." *Howard Journal of Communications* 31, no. 1 (January): 35–49. https://doi.org/10.1080/10646175.2019.1590256.

McClintock, Anne. 2013. *Imperial Leather: Race, Gender, and Sexuality in the Colonial Contest*. Hoboken: Taylor and Francis. http://www.123library.org/book_details/?id=110215.

McDonald, Soraya Nadia. 2017. "Why Floyd Mayweather Can Still Box after Beating Women." *The Undefeated* (blog), August 23, 2017. https://theundefeated.com/features/why–floyd–mayweather–can–still–box–after–beating–women/.

McGevna, Allison. 2020. "We Don't Need To Destroy Gayle King To Preserve Kobe Bryant's Legacy." *Essence* (blog). December 6, 2020. https://www.essence.com/feature/gayle–king–cbs–kobe–bryant–sexism–misogynoir/.

McGuire, Danielle L. 2010. *At the Dark End of the Street: Black Women, Rape, and Resistance– a New History of the Civil Rights Movement from Rosa Parks to the Rise of Black Power*. 1st ed. New York: Alfred A. Knopf.

Melancon, Trimiko, and Joanne M. Braxton, eds. 2015. *Black Female Sexualities*. New Brunswick: Rutgers University Press.

Mina, An Xiao. 2019. *Memes to Movements: How the World's Most Viral Media Is Changing Social Protest and Power*. Boston: Beacon Press.

Mitchell, Mary. 2015. "Fox's 'Empire' Revives 'Blaxploitation' Genre." *Chicago Sun–Times*, January 26, 2015. https://chicago.suntimes.com/entertainment–and–culture/2015/1/26/18574468/fox–s–empire–revives–blaxploitation–genre.

Moffit, Kimberly. 2020. "Light–Skinned People Always Win: An Auto–Ethnography of Colorism in a Mother–Daughter Relationship." *Women, Gender and Families of Color* 8, no. 1 (Spring): 65–86.

Molina–Guzmán, Isabel. 2016. "#OscarsSoWhite: How Stuart Hall Explains Why Nothing Changes in Hollywood and Everything Is Changing." *Critical Studies in Media Communication* 33, no. 5 (October): 438–54. https://doi.org/10.1080/15295036.2016.1227864.

Moore, Mignon R. 2008. "Gendered Power Relations among Women: A Study of Household Decision Making in Black, Lesbian Stepfamilies." *American Sociological Review* 73, no. 2 (April): 335–56. https://doi.org/10.1177/000312240807300208.

Moreno, Carolina. 2018. "Junot Díaz: The African Diaspora 'Doesn't Look the Way It Looks without Systematic Rape.'" *HuffPost*, February 9, 2018. https://www.huffpost.com/entry/junot–diazafrican–diaspora–systematic–rape_n_5a7dbbefe4b08dfc9303693f.

Morgan, Joan. 2000. *When Chickenheads Come Home to Roost: A Hip–Hop Feminist Breaks It Down*. New York: Simon and Shuster. Kindle.

Morris, Angelica, and Lee Ann Kahlor. 2018. "Intensifying the Burden: The Implications of Individual Responsibility Messages in HIV Public Service Announcements Aimed at Black Women." *Sex Education* 18, no. 5 (August): 571–86.

Morrison, Tawana Jones. 2020. "Who Are My Sisters' Keepers?" Ms. Magazine. June 9, 2020. https://msmagazine.com/2020/06/09/black–women–girls–who–are–my–sisters–keepers/.

MSNBC.com. 2015. "Megyn Kelly: 'The Girl Was No Saint Either.'" June 9, 2015. https://www.msnbc.com/msnbc–quick–cuts/watch/megyn–kelly–on–mckinney–teen–the–girl–was–no–saint–either–460529731613.

Mulvey, L. 1975. "Visual Pleasure and Narrative Cinema." *Screen* 16, no. 3 (September): 6–18. https://doi.org/10.1093/screen/16.3.6.

Muñoz, José Esteban. 1999. *Disidentifications: Queers of Color and the Performance of Politics*. Cultural Studies of the Americas, v. 2. Minneapolis: University of Minnesota Press.

Ndedi, Alain Aime. 2020. "Framework in Ending Gender–Based Violence with the Advent of the Covid 19 from an African Perspective." *SSRN Electronic Journal*. April 9, 2020. https://doi.org/10.2139/ssrn.3571319.

Neely, Cheryl L. 2015. *You're Dead——so What? Media, Police, and the Invisibility of Black Women as Victims of Homicide*. East Lansing: Michigan State University Press.

New York Film Academy. 2018. "Gender Inequality in Film Infographic by the New York Film Academy Updated in 2018.". https://www.nyfa.edu/nyfa–news/gender–inequality–in–film–infographic–by–nyfa–updated–in–2018.php#.X5tU1lNKjPY.

Nills, Billy. 2019. "Everything That's Happened Since Surviving R. Kelly Rocked R. Kelly's World—and What's Next for the Disgraced Star," *E! Online.* May 4, 2019. https://www.eonline.com/news/1038110/everything–that–s–happened–since–surviving–r–kelly–rocked–r–kelly–s–world–and–what–s–next–for–the–disgraced–star.

Noble, Safiya Umoja. 2018. *Algorithms of Oppression: How Search Engines Reinforce Racism*. New York: New York University Press.

———. 2019. "Toward a Critical Black Digital Humanities." In *Debates in the Digital Humanities 2019*, edited by Matthew K. Gold and Lauren F. Klein, 27–35. University of Minnesota Press. https://doi.org/10.5749/j.ctvg251hk.5.

Norwalk, Peter. *How to Get Away with Murder*. ABC Studios, 2014 – 2020.

Omi, Michael, and Howard Winant. 2015. *Racial Formation in the United States*. Third edition. New York: Routledge/Taylor & Francis Group.

Oware, Matthew. 2011. "Brotherly Love: Homosociality and Black Masculinity in Gangsta Rap Music." *Journal of African American Studies* 15, no. 1 (March): 22–39. https://doi.org/10.1007/s12111–010–9123–4.

Owen, David. 2017. *Player and Avatar: The Affective Potential of Videogames*. Studies in Gaming. Jefferson, North Carolina: McFarland & Company, Inc.

Owens, Timothy. 2003. *Handbook of Self and Identity*. Edited by Mark R. Leary and June Price Tangney. New York: Guilford Press.

Page, Helan E. 1997. "'Black Male' Imagery and Media Containment of African American Men." *American Anthropologist* 99, no. 1 (March): 99–111. https://doi.org/10.1525/aa.1997.99.1.99.

Parham, Jason. 2015. "Inside the World of the Black Elite: An Interview With Margo Jefferson." *Gawker*. September 29, 2015. http://review.gawker.com/inside–the–world–of–americas–black–elite–an–interview–1733411276.

Parks, Sheri. 2013. *Fierce Angels: Living with a Legacy from the Sacred Dark Feminine to the Strong Black Woman*. New expanded edition. Chicago, Illinois: Lawrence Hill Books.

Patterson–Faye, Courtney J. 2016. "'I like the Way You Move': Theorizing Fat, Black and Sexy." *Sexualities* 19, no. 8 (December): 926–44. https://doi.org/10.1177/1363460716640731.

Patterson, Robert J. 2011. ""Woman Thou Art Bound"': Critical Spectatorship, Black Masculine Gazes, and Gender Problems in Tyler Perry's Movies." *Black Camera* 3, no. 1 (Winter): 9–30. https://doi.org/10.2979/blackcamera.3.1.9.

Payne, Ashley. 2020. "The Cardi B–Beyoncé Complex: Ratchet Respectability and Black Adolescent Girlhood." *Journal of Hip–Hop Studies. Vol. 7*, 2020, Issue 1 (July). https://doi.org/10.34718/PXEW–7785.

Pennolino, Paul, Director. 1996. *The Daily Show*. Comedy Central, 1996–Present.

Petersen, Emily E., Nicole L. Davis, David Goodman, et.al. 2019. "Racial/Ethnic Disparities in Pregnancy–Related Deaths — United States, 2007–2016." *MMWR. Morbidity and Mortality Weekly Report* 68, no. 35 (September): 762–65. https://doi.org/10.15585/mmwr.mm6835a3.

Peterson, Carla L. n.d. "Family." *Keywords for American Cultural Studies, Second Edition*." New York: NYU Press. Online. https://keywords.nyupress.org/american–cultural–studies/essay/family/.

Plencner, A. 2014. "Critical Thinking and the Challenges of Internet." *Communication Today* 5, no. 2 (December): 4–19.

Quinn, Eithne. 2013. "Black Talent and Conglomerate Hollywood: Will Smith, Tyler Perry, and the Continuing Significance of Race." *Popular Communication* 11, no. 3 (July): 196–210. https://doi.org/10.1080/15405702.2013.810070.

Randolph, Antonia. 2018. "When Men Give Birth to Intimacy: The Case of Jay–Z's '4:44.'" *Journal of African American Studies* 22, no. 4 (December): 393–406. https://doi.org/10.1007/s12111–018–9418–4.

Ray, Victor, and Louise Seamster. 2018. "Against Teleology in the Study of Race: Toward the Abolition of the Progress Paradigm." *Sociological Theory* 36, no. 4 (December): 315–42. https://doi.org/10.1177/0735275118813614.

Ray, Victor Erik, Antonia Randolph, Megan Underhill, and David Luke. 2017. "Critical Race Theory, Afro–Pessimism, and Racial Progress Narratives." *Sociology of Race and Ethnicity* 3, no. 2 (April): 147–58. https://doi.org/10.1177/2332649217692557.

Redmond, Shana L. 2013. *Anthem: Social Movements and the Sound of Solidarity in the African Diaspora*. New York: NYU Press.

Retta, Mary. 2020. "Breonna Taylor's Memory Is Being Disrespected Online." *Bitch Media*. July 9, 2020. https://www.bitchmedia.org/article/breonna–taylor–memes–are–disrespecting–her–memory.

Rhor, Monica. 2019. "Pushed out and Punished: One Woman's Story Shows How Systems Are Failing Black Girls." *USA Today*. May 14, 2019. https://www.usatoday.com/in–depth/news/nation/2019/05/13/racism–black–girls–school–discipline–juvenile–court–system–child–abuse–incarceration/3434742002/.

Risam, Roopika. 2015. "Toxic Femininity 4.0." *First Monday*, 20 no. (April): 4 –6 http://doi.org/10.5210/fm.v20i4.5896

Ritchie, Andrea J. 2019. "How a Violent, Viral Arrest Changed Dajerria Becton's Life." *Teen Vogue*. June 19, 2019. https://www.teenvogue.com/story/dajerria–becton–arrest–pool–party–viral.

———. 2017. *Invisible No More: Police Violence against Black Women and Women of Color*. Boston: Beacon Press.

Robinson, Cedric J. 1983. *Black Marxism: The Making of the Black Radical Tradition*. Chapel Hill: The University of North Carolina Press.

Robinson, Petra, Ayana Allen–Handy, and Kala Burrell–Craft. 2021. "Critical Media Literacy and Black Female Identity Construction: A Conceptual Framework for Empowerment, Equity, and Social Justice in Education." *Journal of Media Literacy Education* 13, no. 1 (May): 79–91. https://doi.org/https://doi.org/10.23860/JMLE–2021–13–1–7.

Ryder, Taryn. 2020. "#GirlDad Goes Viral after ESPN Anchor Elle Duncan's Emotional Kobe Bryant Tribute." *Yahoo.com*. January 28, 2020. https://www.yahoo.com/entertainment/girldad–viral–espn–anchor–elle–duncan–kobe–bryant–tribute–174356320.html.

Schiappa, Edward. 2008. *Beyond Representational Correctness: Rethinking Criticism of Popular Media*. Albany: State University of New York Press.

See Jane. nd. "Research Informs & Empowers." Accessed October 29, 2020. https://seejane.org/research–informs–empowers/.

Sharpe, Christina Elizabeth. 1999. "Racialized Fantasies on the Internet." *Signs* 24, no. 4 (Summer): 1089–96. https://www.jstor.org/stable/3175605.

Shearer, Elisa, and Jeffrey Gottfried. 2017. "News Use Across Social Media Platforms 2017." *Pew Research Center's Journalism Project* (blog), September 7, 2017. https://www.journalism.org/2017/09/07/news–use–across–social–media–platforms–2017/.

Shohat, Ella, and Robert Stam. 1994. *Unthinking Eurocentrism: Multiculturalism and the Media*. New York: Routledge.

Shugerman, Emily. 2019. "Sex Abuse Hotline Calls Surge During 'Surviving R.Kelly.'" *The Daily Beast*, January 4, 2019. https://www.thedailybeast.com/sex–abuse–hotline–calls–surge–during–lifetimes–surviving–rkelly.

Shuy, Roger W. 2012. *The Language of Sexual Misconduct Cases*. New York: Oxford University Press.

Simonton, Dean Keith. 2009. "Cinematic Success Criteria and Their Predictors: The Art and Business of the Film Industry." *Psychology and Marketing* 26, no. 5 (May): 400–420. https://doi.org/10.1002/mar.20280.

Sims, David. 2016. "'Insecure' Is Quietly Revolutionary." *The Atlantic*, October 8, 2016. https://www.theatlantic.com/entertainment/archive/2016/10/insecure–hbo–review/503363/.

Smith, Andrea. 2016. "Heteropatriarchy and the Three Pillars of White Supremacy: Rethinking Women of Color Organizing." In *Color of Violence*, edited by INCITE: Women of Color Against Violence, 66–73. Durham: Duke University Press. https://doi.org/10.1215/9780822373445–007.

Smith, Shawn Michelle. 1999. *American Archives: Gender, Race, and Class in Visual Culture*. Princeton, N.J: Princeton University Press.

Snider, Idrissa. 2018. "'Girl Bye: Turning from Stereotypes to Self–Defined Images, A Womanist Exploration on Crooked Room Analysis.'" *Kaleidoscope: A Graduate Journal of Qualitative Communication Research* 17, no. 1 (n.d.). https://opensiuc.lib.siu.edu/kaleidoscope/vol17/iss1/3.

Sobande, Francesca. 2019. "How to Get Away with Authenticity: Viola Davis and the Intersections of Blackness, Naturalness, Femininity and Relatability." *Celebrity Studies* 10, no. 3 (July 3, 2019): 396–410. https://doi.org/10.1080/19392397.2019.1630154.

Sperling, Nicole. 2020, "Academy Explains Diversity Rules for Best Picture Oscar." *The New York Times*, September 8, 2020, sec. Movies. https://www.nytimes.com/2020/09/08/movies/oscars–diversity–rules–best–picture.html.

Stern, Robin. 2007. *The Gaslight Effect: How to Spot and Survive the Hidden Manipulations Other People Use to Control Your Life*. 1st ed. New York: Morgan Road Books, 2007.

Stewart, Pearl. 2007. "Who Is Kin?: Family Definition and African American Families." *Journal of Human Behavior in the Social Environment* 15, no. 2–3 (November): 163–81. https://doi.org/10.1300/J137v15n02_10.

Stoddard, Jeremy D., and Alan S. Marcus. 2006. "The Burden of Historical Representation: Race, Freedom, "Educational" Hollywood Film." *Film & History: An Interdisciplinary Journal of Film and Television Studies* 36, no. 1 (2006): 26–35. https://doi.org/10.1353/flm.2006.0018.

Stump, Scott. 2020. "Kobe Bryant Loved Being a 'Girl Dad,' and This Touching Story Explains Why." *TODAY.com*. January 28, 2020. https://www.today.com/parents/kobe–bryant–loved–being–girl–dad–elle–duncan–s–touching–t172626.

Stone, Robin. 2007. *No Secrets No Lies: How Black Families Can Heal from Sexual Abuse*. New York: Broadway Books. Kindle.

Storer, Heather L., Allison Talan, Alison Swiatlo, Kendra LeSar, Marsha Broussard, Carl Kendall, David W. Seal, and Aubrey Spriggs Madkour. 2020. "Context Matters:

Factors That Influence African American Teens' Perceptions and Definitions of Dating Violence." *Psychology of Violence* 10, no. 1 (January): 79–90. https://doi.org/10.1037/vio0000232.

Stuever, Hank. 2018. "After All the Praise and Hype, What If 'Atlanta' Is Just a Great Show about the Human Condition?" *Washington Post*. February 28, 2018. https://www.washingtonpost.com/entertainment/tv/after–all–the–praise–and–hype–what–if–atlanta–is–just–a–great–show–about–the–human–condition/2018/02/28/92878d66–1bec–11e8–ae5a–16e60e4605f3_story.html.

Swartz, David. 1998. *Culture and Power: The Sociology of Pierre Bourdieu*. Chicago: University of Chicago Press. http://qut.eblib.com.au/patron/FullRecord.aspx?p=3038498.

Tally, Margaret. 2016. *The Rise of the Anti–Heroine in TV's Third Golden Age*. Newcastle upon Tyne: Cambridge Scholars Publishing.

Tasker, Yvonne. 2015. *The Hollywood Action and Adventure Film*. 1st ed. New Approaches to Film Genre. Malden, MA: Wiley–Blackwell.

Taylor, Keeanga–Yamahtta. 2020. "Until Black Women Are Free, None of Us Will Be Free." *The New Yorker*. July 20, 2020. https://www.newyorker.com/news/our–columnists/until–black–women–are–free–none–of–us–will–be–free.

———. 2017. *How We Get Free: Black Feminism and the Combahee River Collective*. Chicago: Haymarket Books.

Taylor, Ula Y. 2017. *The Promise of Patriarchy: Women and the Nation of Islam*. The John Hope Franklin Series in African American History and Culture. Chapel Hill: The University of North Carolina Press.

Tener, Dafna. 2018. "The Secret of Intrafamilial Child Sexual Abuse: Who Keeps It and How?" *Journal of Child Sexual Abuse* 27, no. 1 (January): 1–21. https://doi.org/10.1080/10538712.2017.1390715.

Thomas, Jamescia. 2016. "Black Girl Magic Is More than a Hashtag." *CNN*. February 24, 2016. https://www.cnn.com/2016/02/24/living/black–girl–magic–feat/index.html.

Torres, Sasha. 2003. *Black, White, and in Color: Television and Black Civil Rights*. Princeton: Princeton University Press.

Towns, Armond R. 2016. "Geographies of Pain: #SayHerName and the Fear of Black Women's Mobility." *Women's Studies in Communication* 39, no. 2 (April): 122–26. https://doi.org/10.1080/07491409.2016.1176807.

Tsivian, Yuri. 2013. *Early Cinema in Russia and Its Cultural Reception*. New York: Routledge.

Turnage, Barbara F. 2004. "African American Mother–Daughter Relationships Mediating Daughter's Self–Esteem." *Child and Adolescent Social Work Journal* 21, no. 2 (April): 155–73. https://doi.org/10.1023/B:CASW.0000022729.07706.fc.

Ugwu, Reggie. 2019. "(Hollywood) 'They Set Us Up to Fail.'" *The New York Times*, July 3, 2019. https://www.nytimes.com/2019/07/03/movies/black–directors–1990s.html

USAID. "United States Strategy to Prevent and Respond to Gender–Based Violence Globally 2016 Update." U.S. Agency for International Development. March 11, 2019. https://www.usaid.gov/gbv.

Valencia Jones, Lani, and Beverly Guy–Sheftall. 2015. "Conquering the Black Girl Blues." *Social Work* 60, no. 4 (October): 343–50. https://doi.org/10.1093/sw/swv032.

Vass, Victoria, Katarzyna Sitko, Sophie West, and Richard P. Bentall. 2017. "How Stigma Gets under the Skin: The Role of Stigma, Self–Stigma and Self–Esteem in Subjective Recovery from Psychosis." *Psychosis* 9, no. 3 (July 3): 235–44. https://doi.org/10.1080/17522439.2017.1300184.

Vilanova, John. 2018. "John Legend's EGOT and the Seduction of Symbolic Racial Progress." *The Atlantic*, September 14, 2018. https://www.theatlantic.com/entertainment/archive/2018/09/john–legends–egot–and–the–seduction–of–symbolic–racial–progress/570058/.

Villi, Mikko, and Janne Matikainen. 2016. "Participation in Social Media: Studying Explicit and Implicit Forms of Participation in Communicative Social Networks." *Media and Communication* 4, no. 4 (October): 109–17. https://doi.org/10.17645/mac.v4i4.578.

Voytko, Lisette. 2020. "'Not Messing Around': Oscars' New Diversity Rules Draw Praise And Criticism." *Forbes*. September 9, 2020. https://www.forbes.com/sites/lisettevoytko/2020/09/09/not–messing–around–oscars–new–diversity–rules–draw–praise–and–criticism/.

Wacquant, Loïc J. D. 2009. *Punishing the Poor: The Neoliberal Government of Social Insecurity*. Politics, History, and Culture. Durham: Duke University Press.

Waite, L. J., E. O. Laumann, A. Das, and L. P. Schumm. 2009. "Sexuality: Measures of Partnerships, Practices, Attitudes, and Problems in the National Social Life, Health, and Aging Study." *The Journals of Gerontology Series B: Psychological Sciences and Social Sciences* 64B, no. Supplement 1 (November): i56–66. https://doi.org/10.1093/geronb/gbp038.

Wallis, Cara. 2011. "Performing Gender: A Content Analysis of Gender Display in Music Videos." *Sex Roles* 64, no. 3–4 (February): 160–72. https://doi.org/10.1007/s11199–010–9814–2.

Walsh, Rebecca M., Amanda L. Forest, and Edward Orehek. 2020. "Self–Disclosure on Social Media: The Role of Perceived Network Responsiveness." *Computers in Human Behavior* 104 (March): 106162. https://doi.org/10.1016/j.chb.2019.106162.

Wanzo, Rebecca Ann. 2009. *The Suffering Will Not Be Televised: African American Women and Sentimental Political Storytelling*. Albany: State University of New York Press.

Waytz, Adam, Kelly Marie Hoffman, and Sophie Trawalter. 2015. "A Superhumanization Bias in Whites' Perceptions of Blacks." *Social Psychological and Personality Science* 6, no. 3 (April): 352–59. https://doi.org/10.1177/1948550614553642.

Weinstone, Ann. 2003. *Avatar Bodies: A Tantra for Posthumanism*. Minneapolis: University of Minnesota Press.

Wells, Dominic D. 2018. "You All Made Dank Memes: Using Internet Memes to Promote Critical Thinking." *Journal of Political Science Education* 14, no. 2 (April): 240–48. https://doi.org/10.1080/15512169.2017.1406363.

West, Carolyn M. 1995. "Mammy, Sapphire, and Jezebel: Historical Images of Black Women and Their Implications for Psychotherapy." *Psychotherapy:*

Theory, Research, Practice, Training 32, no. 3 (Fall): 458–66. https://doi. org/10.1037/0033–3204.32.3.458.

Williams, Serena. 2018. "Serena Williams: What My Life–Threatening Experience Taught Me about Giving Birth." *CNN.* February 20, 2018. https://www.cnn. com/2018/02/20/opinions/protect–mother–pregnancy–williams–opinion/index. html.

Wilkinson, Alissa. 2020, "Do the Oscars' New Rules Mean No More Movies about White People?" *Vox,* September 9, 2020. https://www.vox.com/ culture/2020/9/9/21429083/oscars–best–picture–rules–diversity–inclusion.

Wriggins, Jennifer. 1983. "Rape, Racism, and the Law." *Harvard Women's Law Journal* 6 (January): 103. https://digitalcommons.mainelaw.maine.edu/ faculty–publications/51.

Wright, Michelle M. 2005. "Finding a Place in Cyberspace: Black Women, Technology, and Identity." *Frontiers: A Journal of Women Studies* 26, no. 1 (2005): 48–59. https://www.jstor.org/stable/4137433.

Yancy, George. 2016. *Black Bodies, White Gazes: The Continuing Significance of Race in America.* Second Edition. Lanham: Rowman & Littlefield.

Young, Harvey. 2010. *Embodying Black Experience: Stillness, Critical Memory, and the Black Body.* Theater: Theory/Text/Performance. Ann Arbor: University of Michigan Press.

Young, Kalima. 2016. "We Will Survive: Race and Gender Based Trauma as Cultural Truth Telling." In *Feminist Perspectives on Orange Is the New Black: Thirteen Critical Essays,* edited by April Kalogeropoulos Householder and Adrienne M. Trier–Bieniek. Jefferson, 32–44. North Carolina: McFarland & Company, Inc., Publishers.

Young, Kalima and Kim, Sharon. 2020. "Empathetic Witnessing of Violent Viral Videos." The Pennsylvania Psychologist, 80 no.5 (September): 13–14.

Index

About the Author

Kalima Young is Assistant Professor in the Department of Electronic Media and Film at Towson University. She received her PhD in American Studies from the University of Maryland College Park. Her research explores the impact of race and gender-based trauma on Black identity, media, and cultural production. A Baltimore native, videographer, and activist, Dr. Young is also a member of Rooted, a Black LGBTQ healing collective in Baltimore, MD.